COMMON SENSE
ON WEAPONS
OF MASS
DESTRUCTION

COMMON SENSE
ON WEAPONS
OF MASS
DESTRUCTION

Ambassador Thomas Graham Jr.

UNIVERSITY OF WASHINGTON PRESS
SEATTLE & LONDON
IN ASSOCIATION WITH THE
EISENHOWER INSTITUTE
WASHINGTON, D.C.

For Christine

University of Washington Press
P.O. Box 50096, Seattle, WA 98145, U.S.A.
www.washington.edu/uwpress

Library of Congress Cataloging-in-Publication Data
Graham, Thomas.
Common sense on weapons of mass destruction /
Thomas Graham Jr. — 1st ed.
p. cm.
Includes index.
ISBN 0-295-98466-x (pbk. : alk. paper)
1. Nuclear nonproliferation.   2. Weapons of mass destruction.
3. Arms control.   4. Security, International.   I. Title.
JZ5675.G73   2004
327.1'745 — dc22   2004016020

The paper used in this publication is acid-free and recycled
from 20 percent post-consumer and at least 50 percent pre-consumer
waste. It meets the minimum requirements of American National
Standard for Information Sciences-Permanence of Paper for
Printed Library Materials, ANSI Z39.48-1984.

Contents

Foreword

I COMMEND AMBASSADOR GRAHAM FOR WRITING this much-needed book. Nuclear weapons in the hands of "rogue" states or terrorist organizations represent the principal security threat to the United States and to the world community today. The aftermath of the Cold War has in many ways left us less secure, given the large numbers of unnecessary and dangerous nuclear weapons, the enormous stockpiles of nuclear bomb material in Russia and elsewhere, and the spread of other types of weapons of mass destruction. It is to nuclear weapons that we must turn our principal attention—only they can cripple civilization as we know it.

Our principal bulwark against the threat represented by the current number and potential proliferation of nuclear weapons is the Nuclear Non-Proliferation Treaty (NPT). Some argue that the NPT has failed and has become irrelevant, and that the only counter to nuclear proliferation is unilateral force—a course which history tells us is counterproductive at best, and probably disastrous. But the NPT regime has not failed. Only two more countries have nuclear weapons now than had them in 1970 when the NPT entered into force. However, the International Atomic Energy Agency estimates that sixty to seventy countries are now capable of building nuclear weapons. Should a substantial number of states act on this capability (as was predicted years ago before the NPT was signed), it would create a world far different from the one that we have now, and one that it is difficult even to contemplate. It would be a world in which the stability of civilization would continually remain in the balance.

But this can be avoided and nuclear nonproliferation policies can continue to prevail if the NPT regime is strictly observed by all states — this means by all states, including the five nuclear weapon states: the United States, Britain, France, Russia, and China. The NPT was created in 1970 on the basis of a mutual commitment, expressed in Article 6 of the treaty, that in exchange for the rest of the world agreeing not to acquire nuclear weapons, the five nuclear weapon states would engage in nuclear disarmament negotiations aimed at eventually eliminating nuclear weapons and would share peaceful nuclear technology. When the NPT was made permanent in 1995, this commitment was refined to make clear that it included deep reductions leading toward the elimination of nuclear weapons and support for a comprehensive nuclear test ban treaty. It also meant strict observance of the promises by the nuclear weapon states not to use nuclear weapons against nonnuclear NPT parties. The NPT nonnuclear weapon states (now numbering 182) have always been skeptical about NPT compliance by the nuclear weapon states, and they are presently far more skeptical as a result of the United States backing away from treaty commitments in recent years. It is correct to emphasize the importance of compliance with the NPT regime as the White House has done. Actions are urgently needed to ensure the long-term viability of the NPT, which is absolutely essential to peace and security in the twenty-first century. I suggest we proceed along the following lines:

If the NPT nuclear weapon states would agree to a plan whereby truly drastic reductions in nuclear weapons would be achieved over a period of years, then the Security Council could agree that any breach of the nonnuclear status of any of the 182 NPT nonnuclear weapon states would be regarded as a breach of the peace, with the council agreeing in advance that if it should determine that proliferation had taken place, "all necessary means" (including conventional military force) would be authorized to correct the situation. As part of this, all of the states possessing nuclear weapons would be required to declare in a submission to the council their number and type. Then the United States and Russia could agree to a very low residual level of nuclear weapons in the range of 50 to 100 each, with Britain, France, and China reducing to a level just above elimination. In return for eliminating their nuclear weapon programs, India, Pakistan, Israel, and North Korea would receive from the permanent members of the Security Council (the United States, Russia, France, Britain, and China) legally binding security guarantees against attack. The nonnuclear weapon states would pledge again their nonnuclear status and agree to support a call for force by the Security Council against any violator. This is the kind of outcome we must pursue if peace and security in the new century is to have a chance.

This subject is simply and carefully presented in Ambassador Graham's book. Before we can have sensible policies toward nuclear weapons and other problems left over from the Cold War, there must be public understanding. Only with the support and indeed the insistence of the public can governments begin to effectively follow policies designed to make the world a more peaceful place. This book makes a most important contribution to this: it makes this complicated process approachable. I recommend Ambassador Graham's book to all those who care about the future of our country, and indeed the world.

ROBERT S. MCNAMARA

COMMON SENSE
ON WEAPONS
OF MASS
DESTRUCTION

Introduction

EVERY FOUR YEARS, THE CHICAGO COUNCIL ON Foreign Relations conducts a public survey of American attitudes toward foreign policy issues, a poll considered to be the most authoritative on this subject. In the poll released in 2000, Americans identified nuclear weapon proliferation (the spread of nuclear weapons to countries that don't presently have them) as more serious than any other issue. Year after year, poll results indicate that the American public understands the dangers of nuclear weapon proliferation and nuclear terrorism; supports the Nuclear Non-Proliferation Treaty (NPT), which has effectively restrained the spread of nuclear weapons since its inception in 1970; favors U.S. ratification of the Comprehensive Nuclear-Test-Ban Treaty (CTBT); supports significant reductions in nuclear weapons; and recognizes the importance of the rule of international law. But the American public's positions are rarely translated into policy in Washington. What is the reason for this?

After the October 1999 vote in the U.S. Senate refusing to

endorse the CTBT for ratification, a poll found that two-thirds of respondents opposed what the Senate had done, but only one-third said that the position of their two senators on this issue would affect their vote for either one when seeking reelection. Arms control, nonproliferation, and international law are a significant component of national security; Americans know this, and know how important a united world community is in defending against the threat of international terrorism, yet these issues are far down on their list of priorities when it comes to electing individuals to national public offices. This is so even though the overwhelming majority of Americans understand the danger that vast numbers of weapons of mass destruction (particularly nuclear weapons) present, and how uncertain their security and world security are as a result.

One reason for this seeming lack of active public support is that arms control, nonproliferation, and international law seem complicated, technical, difficult to understand, and removed from everyday life. Another reason may be that with the end of the Cold War (the era of thermonuclear confrontation between the two superpowers), the decline in world order, and the rise of international terrorism, these issues may seem less relevant than they once were. This book argues that arms control, nonproliferation, and international law are in fact accessible to the general public, and that they are just as, if not more, relevant than ever.

In the wake of two horrifically destructive world wars, the United States has led the world toward a more stable and orderly condition based on successful Cold War alliances and a vast international security treaty structure. The United States was the principal creator of the United Nations and the prime mover in establishing this international treaty structure, the centerpiece of which is the Nuclear Non-Proliferation Treaty, signed in 1968. This treaty and the many other agreements associated with or derived from it have largely contained the spread of nuclear weapons and have helped to establish strategic stability among the countries of the world. Additionally, by means of related agreements, chemical and biological weapons have been outlawed, nuclear weapon delivery vehicles (missiles and bombers) have been controlled, and conventional weapons (tanks, artillery, and landmines) have been limited. All of these agreements bolstered peace and stability in the latter half of the twentieth century, and will likely continue to do so in the twenty-first century. But in recent years, the United States has failed to provide global leadership in support of international law and the international treaty structure. As a result, this treaty structure is eroding and, most worrisome of all, the NPT itself has come under heavy pressure. It would be catastrophic should the NPT fall apart and nuclear weapons begin to spread around the world.

Nuclear weapons and nuclear deterrence played an important role during the Cold War, but given the world today, and the threats that face us — international terrorism, unstable states, and the proliferation of weapons of mass destruction, which include nuclear, chemical, and biological weapons and their delivery systems — it is of the highest urgency to preserve and strengthen international cooperation and international treaty arrangements. Nuclear weapons have a very limited role to play in this effort: that of deterring their use by others. In order to discourage states from wishing to acquire them today, nuclear weapons should be de-emphasized and reduced to the lowest level consistent with safety, stability, and security.

This is not a universal view. It has not been the view of any administration in office as of yet. Many thousands of nuclear weapons still remain deployed in the field on hair-trigger alert more than ten years after the end of the Cold War. The possession of nuclear weapons still affects a state's international standing, and nuclear weapons are still highly valued by the states that have them. This situation needs to begin to change if the NPT and the associated treaty structure are to survive and peace and stability are to be achieved in the twenty-first century.

Many are not yet convinced of the necessity of nuclear weapon reductions. They worry about verification. Is it possible to know with accuracy how many nuclear weapons another state has? They are also concerned about stability at lower weapon levels, where the acquisition of a few more weapons could make a great difference. The verification technologies available today answer the first concern in the affirmative, and, as for the second, stability and deterrence are just as possible at low levels as at high levels (hundreds rather than thousands of nuclear weapons) now that the Cold War is over. Of course, agreed verification arrangements would have to go far beyond any that have been made thus far, and would have to be based on cooperative principles.

For example, restricting the United States and Russia to three hundred weapons each, as recommended by the 1997 National Academy of Sciences report *The Role of Nuclear Weapons*, would provide as much stability as the tens of thousands of nuclear weapons deployed during the Cold War, or the many thousands deployed today. There is no need to target the enormous number of facilities that were targeted during the Cold War. With today's nonconfrontational relationship between the United States and Russia, three hundred weapons (more than either the United States or Russia could realistically ever find targets for) would be entirely sufficient for whatever deterrence is still required. And the reduction by Britain, France, and China to very low levels (below 100 each) also would have no effect on stability or deterrence. These three states have minimum nuclear deterrent postures, and 80 to 90 nuclear weapons would be more than sufficient for one of them to discourage any threat of nuclear attack (as reflected in the National Academy study). Reducing to these levels would devalue nuclear weapons as great power symbols and thereby greatly strengthen the NPT. No matter how important one considers the maintenance of nuclear deterrence, in today's world, where the problem is not the confrontation of superpowers but rather rogue states, terrorists, and proliferation, stable numbers of weapons at much lower levels is more secure.

Some argue, however, that while nuclear deterrence no longer has a significant role to play, neither do nuclear nonproliferation agreements, because rogue states cheat on the agreements and terrorists are not bound by them. Rather, it is asserted, the United States should rely on a unilateralist preemptive policy of counter-proliferation using military force when necessary. But the failure of intelligence to accurately portray the situation in Saddam Hussein's Iraq points up the danger of relying on a preemptive strategy where much is unknowable, and the threat of possible nuclear weapon programs in North Korea and Iran underscores the difficulty of the United States going it alone. It is clear that both of these conflicts can be effectively resolved only through the cooperation and consistent effective effort of the international community (in the case of North Korea, with special emphasis on states in that region). And there can only be consistent effective international action through a treaty system such as the NPT regime, which requires cooperation. Thus, strong and viable arms control and nonproliferation treaty systems are as essential to peace and stability today as they have ever been.

This is a subject the American people must take seriously. The terrible tragedy of the terrorist attacks on September 11, 2001, underscored the dangerous nature of the world today and the importance of national security issues. Americans have always supported defense programs that they believe are necessary for their security, as well as arms limitation arrangements that make for a safer world. But it has been much easier to translate the support for defense programs into support for candidates espousing them than has been the case with arms limitation measures.

Defense programs are finite and they produce jobs; arms limitation measures are often esoteric, difficult to define, and do not as often lead to concrete results — rather, they prevent things from happening.

A note about the organization of this book: Two subjects, nuclear-weapon reductions and missile proliferation, do not have separate chapters. The first of these two subjects is subsumed in Chapters 5 and 7 as directly relevant to the political value of nuclear weapons and to missile defense policies. The second subject relates to both missile defense and outer space security. A discussion of missile proliferation is included in Chapter 7, as it has the most direct bearing on this subject.

Finally, while emphasizing the threat of nuclear proliferation, this book addresses other relevant issues, such as missile defense, the weaponization of space, regional issues, chemical and biological weapons, and the proliferation of small arms. All of these are related to the central question of international terrorism, unstable states, a decline in world order, and loose WMDs.

1

The Problems of Our Time: Nuclear Proliferation and Nuclear Terrorism

D ISARMAMENT AND ARMS CONTROL ARE NOT new. In 1139, at the Second Lateran Council, Pope Innocent II outlawed the crossbow, declaring it to be "hateful to God and unfit for Christians." The crossbow was later overtaken in effectiveness by the English longbow. The crossbow and the longbow were then eclipsed by the destructive firepower of the cannon. The Church also banned the rifle when it appeared, but military technology continued to develop over the centuries, and diplomacy and arms control efforts could not keep pace. This changed with the advent of the atomic bomb in 1945. For the first time, humanity possessed a weapon with which it could destroy itself. Disarmament efforts gradually gained momentum, and over time a web of international treaties and agreements have been constructed that have inhibited the spread of nuclear, chemical, and biological weapons and limited their development.

There is no question but that these efforts have changed the course of history.

Nuclear weapons are truly a thing apart. The atomic bomb used against Hiroshima in 1945 was 12.5 kilotons, the equivalent in explosive power of 12,500 tons of TNT. In the mid-1950s, the United States and the Soviet Union were testing nuclear weapons in the megaton range, equivalent to one million tons of TNT. For reference, one megaton roughly compares to a freight train loaded with TNT, stretching from New York to Los Angeles. In the 1960s, the United States deployed (operationally placed in the field) missiles in underground silo launchers around the country, each with a 9-megaton warhead. Just one of these weapons detonated at the Washington Monument could have more or less destroyed Washington, D.C., out to the capital beltway in every direction (an approximately fifteen-mile radius). The United States routinely carried multiple bombs on its B-52 bombers, each with the explosive power of 25 megatons. One of these bombers carried more explosive power than was used by all the sides in World War II. The Soviet Union deployed intercontinental missiles with nuclear warheads comparable to these bomber weapons.

Soon after 1945, a vast nuclear arms race was underway. By the 1960s, it appeared as if nuclear weapons would spread all over the world. There were reports issued in 1962 estimating that by the end of the 1970s there would be twenty-five to thirty states with nuclear weapons integrated into their national arsenals and ready for use. Had this happened, there would likely be more than fifty nuclear weapon states today. This would have created a nightmarish world. Nuclear weapons would be so widespread that it would be impossible to keep them out of the hands of terrorists, and every conflict would run the risk of "going nuclear."

In 1960, when France detonated its first nuclear weapon, the headlines in French newspapers read "Vive la France!" Fourteen years later, India's first nuclear explosion, figuratively conducted in the middle of the night, received worldwide condemnation. What intervened? The Nuclear Non-Proliferation Treaty. The Nuclear Non-Proliferation Treaty (NPT), signed in 1968, entered into force in 1970, and indefinitely extended in 1995, converted what had been an act of national pride (the acquisition of nuclear weapons) into an act considered contrary to the practices of the civilized world. The then five nuclear weapon states (the United States, the Soviet Union, Britain, France, and China) agreed to certain nuclear arms control and disarmament commitments, including deep reductions in nuclear weapons leading to their eventual complete elimination, a ban on nuclear test explosions, and a pledge never to use nuclear weapons against nonnuclear weapon parties. In exchange, most of the rest of the world agreed never to acquire nuclear weapons.

In effect, the NPT made the acquisition of nuclear weapons by countries that joined the NPT as nonnuclear weapon states (currently some 182 countries) a violation of international law. The three states that refused to join the NPT as nonnuclear weapon states and that built nuclear weapons—India, Pakistan, and Israel—are for this reason considered as somewhat outside of the world community, and votes at the United Nations and at international conferences reflect this. India, Pakistan, and Israel were not given the opportunity to join the NPT in 1968 as nuclear weapon states, as they did not then possess (or in Israel's case, claim to possess) nuclear weapons, and the NPT decision was to stop the spread of nuclear weapons where it was at that time. The International Atomic Energy Agency (IAEA), a United Nations–related organization, has estimated that perhaps sixty to seventy nations today possess the capability to build such weapons.

North Korea, which has long been thought to have enough plutonium for one or two bombs, is one such country. By chemically reprocessing the existing spent reactor fuel that it has possessed for years, it could probably make five or six bombs in a few months. Indeed, North Korea claims to have completed the reprocessing and to be building the weapons. Recently, intelligence estimates have appeared in newspapers that say that North Korea may now have up to eight nuclear weapons. This is potentially dangerous, as North Korea has a history of selling its commodities to whomever will buy them. Within recent years, for example, it sold SCUD ballistic missile technology to Iran and Pakistan. An administration source quoted in the *Washington Post* said, in effect, that North Korea's having plutonium for nuclear weapons "fundamentally changes everything" (March 5, 2003). Were North Korea to succeed in making and stockpiling nuclear weapons, "literally, every city on the planet would be threatened," the official said.

North Korea was an NPT party, but withdrew from the treaty early in 2003. Hopefully, North Korea can be persuaded to return to the NPT and to terminate its nuclear weapon program. The only way this can happen is through face-to-face U.S.–North Korean negotiations. Force is not an option. In 1994, during a previous crisis in which the United States threatened to attack its nuclear facilities, North Korea responded that if that we did so, it would turn Seoul (the capitol city of South Korea, with a population of 14 million) into "a sea of fire." In July 2003, North Korea finally agreed to meet with the United States, with other regional powers present (China, Russia, Japan, and South Korea). The first meeting took place in Beijing, China, in August 2003. A second meeting took place in late February 2004. A third meeting was held in May 2004, looking toward a higher-level meeting, which took place in late June 2004. At this meeting, the United States made a comprehensive proposal designed to lead to serious negotiations. North Korea and the United States appear to remain ideologically far apart, but this is a promising development, which should be vigorously and carefully pursued. Nevertheless, a U.S. State Department spokesman said on June 29 that "important differences remain between the parties," indicating that any agreement is still a long way off.

As a nonnuclear party to the NPT, Iran was obligated to sign a safeguards agreement with the IAEA, the purpose of which was to guard against material intended for peaceful nuclear programs being diverted to weapon programs. In December 2003, Iran admitted that it had been in violation of its safeguards agreement with the IAEA for eighteen years, in that it had been developing uranium-enrichment technology without disclosing this to the IAEA. Iran denied any intention of building nuclear weapons, and pledged cooperation with the IAEA in the future. Iran also promised to join the 1997 IAEA expanded inspection protocol (referred to as the Additional Protocol, amending the safeguards agreements) and to "temporarily" halt enrichment activities. Even though Iran did sign the IAEA inspection agreement in December 2003, in early 2004 trace amounts of uranium enriched to weapons grade was found by the IAEA at an Iranian site. In March 2004, Iran was showing signs of beginning to back away from cooperation with the IAEA, and in late June 2004 Iran announced that it was recommencing its construction of uranium-enrichment centrifuge equipment.

In December 2003, Libya announced its decision to eliminate its rudimentary nuclear weapon program as well as its chemical weapon program and to henceforth cooperate with the NPT and the IAEA. An important by-product of this decision was that it exposed the clandestine network headed by Dr. A. Q. Khan, the father of the Pakistani nuclear weapon program, which for many years had been secretly and illegally supplying nuclear weapon technology to Libya, Iran, and North Korea—and perhaps elsewhere. It was claimed that Dr. Khan was acting without the knowledge of Pakistan's military and civilian leaders, although this is not plausible. Dr. Khan publicly apologized and was promptly pardoned by General Pervez Musharraf, the president of Pakistan. However, much of the network is probably still in place.

Iraq's quite serious attempt to acquire nuclear weapons was entirely stifled by the IAEA after the first Gulf War by elimination of the Iraqi infrastructure pursuant to the mandate concluding the war. Despite Iraq's public proclamations to the contrary, its nuclear weapon program was not revived thereafter, in part because of the efficiency of the tight export controls applied to Iraq. Although many believed that the controls had been successful, and the IAEA had asserted as much prior to the second Gulf War, it was not conclusively demonstrated until the summer of 2003, when, after the invasion of Iraq, U.S. inspection teams could find no significant remnant of the Iraqi nuclear weapon program.

As dangerous as North Korea, Iran, and the Pakistani network are in terms of potential nuclear weapon proliferation and nuclear terrorism, just as dangerous is the huge stockpile of fissile material in Russia left over from the Cold War. During the Cold War, according to a former Russian minister of atomic energy, the Russians made 45,000 nuclear weapons and had enough material for 90,000 more. The United States had at one time maintained a level of more than 30,000 nuclear weapons. These efforts bankrupted the Soviet Union and cost the United States in excess of $5.5 trillion (according to a comprehensive study by the Brookings Institution in Washington published in 1998). At the end of the Cold War in 1991, the United States and the Soviet Union agreed, among others things, to eliminate most of their tactical nuclear weapons. The United States has eliminated 95 percent of its tactical nuclear weapons; however, we do not know with any certainty to what degree Russia carried through on this pledge by the Soviet Union. It is not known how many nuclear weapons for short-range or tactical weapon systems they have retained, although it could be many thousands. Present estimates of nuclear weapon levels are in the range of 10,000 for the United States and 15,000 to 20,000 for Russia. This will be discussed further in Chapter 11.

Although Russian weapons are well guarded, their stockpiled highly enriched uranium (HEU) and plutonium are less so. Shortly before I left government in 1997, I had a discussion in Washington with a team of inspectors from the General Accounting Office, the watchdog agency of Congress, who were just back from Russia, where they had been inspecting storage sites for fissile material built with money appropriated by Congress under the Nunn-Lugar program, discussed in Chapter 11. They had visited a storage site in Russia where the HEU was stored in the form of hockey-puck-like wafers stacked in long rows. There were two guards at the facility, with the shift changing every eight hours. The inspectors noticed that when the guards' shifts ended, and the guards went home, they would often slip a "hockey puck" or two into their pockets. An implosion of five such wafers of HEU could devastate a major city.

In 2000, former Senate Majority Leader Howard Baker and prominent Washington lawyer Lloyd Cutler chaired a Department of Energy task force that produced a report on January 10, 2001, that argued that the threat of diversions to dangerous countries and terrorist organizations from the huge stockpile in Russia was so serious, the United States should undertake a crash course to eliminate the stockpile while we still could. They recommended allocating $30 billion to this effort — $3 billion a year for ten years. Over the years, the Congress has been appropriating, and we have been spending about a third of what Baker and Cutler proposed on the problem — $1 billion a year — while we spend $10 billion a year on missile defense to attempt to protect ourselves against what may be the least likely security threat that we face.

On September 11, 2001, with the attacks on the World Trade Center and the Pentagon by terrorist fanatics using passenger airplanes as missiles, the true enemy of the civilized world today—international terrorism fueled by religious and ethnic hatred—unequivocally revealed itself. As horrible as the attacks on the World Trade Center and the Pentagon were, they would have been orders of magnitude worse if a nuclear explosive device had been involved. The threat of nuclear terrorism is growing as technology and materials to build nuclear weapons become more accessible. The "supercomputers" of the 1980s, useful in making atomic weapons and possessed only by a few governments, today can be purchased by anyone. Nuclear weapon technology is sixty years old, and basically no more complicated than a jet engine. The technology used to make the Hiroshima bomb is so simple, a crude weapon made this way does not even need to be tested.

In 1994, while I was leading U.S. government efforts to make the NPT permanent at the upcoming 1995 conference, a colleague and I went to South Africa (which once possessed nuclear weapons) to lobby for their vote. The second day we were there, we were given a tour of the former South African nuclear weapon program infrastructure, which was closed down in the early 1990s. South African Atomic Energy Commission officials took us to the building where the weapons had been assembled. In the very room where the work had been done, they said, "Look around you, nothing has changed since program closure." There was nothing in that room that would not be found in a high school machine shop. They showed us the cases prepared to transport the weapons. They would have easily fit in the back of a panel truck.

After our tour was over, the South African officials told us, "There is a reason we are showing you this. You are the first Americans to see this, except the two on the international inspection team. We built six atomic weapons and had a seventh under way. We never had more than 150 people working directly on this—

including the janitor—and no one knew of it. We used the gun-barrel design, so we didn't need to test the weapons, we knew they would work and would have up to a 20-kiloton yield [50 percent greater than Hiroshima]. If the fissile material can be acquired, the rest is easy. You don't need a big infrastructure. Most countries can do it, and some subnational groups such as sophisticated terrorist organizations or criminal conspiracies could do it. So watch out!"

The United Nations Security Council in 1992 declared proliferation of nuclear weapons to be a "threat to the peace." Prime Minister Tony Blair of Britain, President Jacques Chirac of France, and Chancellor Gerhard Schröder of Germany stated in a joint op-ed article supporting U.S. ratification of the Comprehensive Nuclear-Test-Ban Treaty (*New York Times*, October 18, 1999): "As we look to the next century, our greatest concern is proliferation of weapons of mass destruction, and chiefly nuclear proliferation. We have to face the stark truth that nuclear proliferation remains the major threat to world safety in the twenty-first century." The director-general of the IAEA, Mohamed ElBaradei, said in a speech in Washington in late June 2004, with respect to nuclear proliferation and the possibility of terrorist acquisition of nuclear weapons, "We are actually having a race against time. . . . The danger is so imminent . . . not only with regard to countries acquiring nuclear weapons, but also terrorists getting their hands on some of these nuclear materials—uranium or plutonium" (reported in an editorial in the *Washington Times* on June 25, 2004).

In meeting the threats of international terrorism and weapon proliferation, we must do everything we can to reduce, not enhance, the role of nuclear weapons. This means drastically reducing their numbers, eliminating stockpiles of fissile material, and otherwise strengthening the NPT regime. The difference between U.S. policy toward Iraq (which does not have nuclear weapons) and North Korea (which may) will not be lost on some states—for example, Iran. They may heed the comment made after the first Gulf War, attributed to Krishnaswamy Sundarji, a former chief of staff of the Indian army: "If you are going to take on the United States, you had better have a nuclear weapon." The only effective long-term response to these threats is increased and intensive international cooperation, with an emphasis on international law and specifically the NPT regime. The world community must come together to effectively address the threat of nuclear proliferation, nuclear terrorism, and international security. The nuclear weapon states—most importantly, the United States—should agree to a plan whereby deep reductions in nuclear weapons would be achieved over a period of years, accompanied by far-reaching verification arrangements and information disclosure. Over the long term, the NPT was not intended to be discriminatory, and thus it is important for the long-term viability of the NPT that the NPT nuclear weapon states hold up their side of the bargain. The nonnuclear weapon states should commit themselves again to a nonnuclear status, and agree to an intrusive worldwide inspection program and to support a call for force by the United Nations Security Council against any violator of this new treaty regime. Some appropriate arrangement should be made for the nuclear programs in India, Pakistan, and Israel—for example, reducing their nuclear weapons to zero, but retaining nuclear explosive material on their territory under IAEA safeguards as a hedge against failure of the agreement. In cases such as North Korea's, direct negotiations should be pursued. The huge stockpiles of fissile material (primarily in Russia, but also in the United States) should be reduced as quickly as possible. Drastically reducing the existing number of nuclear weapons and the amount of fissile material to make them would minimize the risk of terrorist acquisition of these weapons. All states should pledge their commitment to the international rule of law and the preeminence of the Security Council in keeping the peace. Such a regime would be a strong contribution to peace, security, and stability for the new century.

This sounds like a tall order, and it is, but we should keep in mind the warning given by Sir Winston Churchill in 1930, as set forth in James C. Humes's book on World War II (*Eisenhower and Churchill: The Partnership that Saved the World*, 2001, p. 16): "It is probabl[e]—nay certain—that among the means which will next time be at their disposal will be agencies and processes of destruction wholesale . . . and perhaps, once launched, uncontrollable. Death stands at attention, obedient, expectant, ready to serve, ready to shear away the peoples en masse, ready, if called on, to pulverize, without hope of repair, what is left of civilization."

2

The Effects of
Nuclear Weapons

I N HIS PULITZER PRIZE−WINNING BOOK *THE
Making of the Atomic Bomb (1986), Richard Rhodes describes
the evolution of the science of nuclear physics that led in less than
fifty years to the atomic bomb. He also describes the actual effects
of using an atomic bomb. The account of the attack on Hiroshima
quoted, summarized, and paraphrased below is found in Chapter 19 of Rhodes's book, "Tongues of Fire."

As Rhodes tells the story, August 6, 1945, began as a beautiful summer day in Hiroshima. The director of the Hiroshima
Communications Hospital began his diary entry of that morning:
"The hour was early, the morning still warm, and beautiful . . .
shimmering leaves, reflecting sunlight from a cloudless sky,
made a pleasant contrast with shadows in my garden." During
the night, some 1,000 miles away, on the island of Tinian in the
Mariana chain, the atomic bomb named "Little Boy" by its design-
ers, carrying a potential explosive power equivalent to 12,500 tons
of TNT, had been loaded onto an American B-29 bomber called

the *Enola Gay*, named after the mother of the pilot, Captain Paul Tibbets. The bomb was ten and one-half feet long, twenty-nine inches in diameter, and weighed approximately four tons. One *Enola Gay* crew member said it looked like "an elongated trash can with fins." Accompanied by escort planes, the American plane left Tinian at 3:00 AM, and was just a few miles from Hiroshima by eight o'clock that morning.

As the American B-29 crossed over the Inland Sea and Hiroshima, a few ships could be seen in the harbor. The bombardier selected as his aim point the Aioi Bridge, a T-shaped bridge spanning the Ota River in central Hiroshima. Tibbets's plane sent out a strong blip on the radio to the escort planes, indicating to them that the bomb would be released in two minutes.

Little Boy exploded at 8:16 AM Hiroshima time, forty-three seconds after it left the *Enola Gay*, 1,900 feet above the courtyard of Shima Hospital, and 550 feet southeast of the Aioi Bridge. As one crew member described it, "Where we had seen a clear city two minutes before, we could no longer see the city. We could see smoke and fire creeping up the sides of the mountains." In the words of another crew member, the city looked like "a pot of boiling black oil." Still another said, "The mushroom was a spectacular sight, a bubbling mass of purple-gray smoke, and you could see it had a red core in it and everything was burning inside."

On the ground, a young girl in the suburbs remembered that "just as I looked up into the sky, there was a flash of white light and the green in the plants looked in that light like the colors of dry leaves." Closer in toward the city, a junior college student recalled that his teacher had had the students look up at the bomber in the sky, and that "we felt a tremendous flash of lightening. In an instant, we were blinded and everything was just a frenzy of delirium." Further in, toward the center of the city, no one survived to remember this light. Rhodes explains that an authoritative Japanese study begun in 1976 in consultation with thirty-four Japanese scientists and physicians concluded that the temperature at the explosion site had reached 5,400°F, and that people within half a mile who had been exposed were burned to bundles of black char in a fraction of a second. Rhodes quotes a patient speaking to that same doctor at Hiroshima Communications Hospital who kept the diary: "A human being who has been roasted becomes quite small, doesn't he?" Rhodes notes that the small black bundles stuck to the streets and bridges and sidewalks of Hiroshima numbered in the thousands.

The Japanese study explained that it was not just human beings that died at Hiroshima:

> In the case of an atomic bombing . . . a community does not merely receive an impact; the community itself is destroyed. Within two kilometers of the atomic bomb's hypocenter, all life and property were shattered, burned, and buried under ashes. The visible forms of the city where people once carried on their daily lives vanished without a trace. The destruction was sudden and thorough; there was virtually no chance to escape . . . citizens who had lost no family members in the holocaust were as rare as stars at sunrise. . . . The atomic bomb had blasted and burned hospitals, schools, city offices, police stations, and every other kind of human organization. . . . Family, relatives, neighbors, and friends relied on a broad range of interdependent organizations for everything from . . . birth, marriage and funerals to firefighting, productive work, and daily living. These traditional communities were completely demolished in an instant.

Rhodes explains that the bomb destroyed not only

> men, women, and thousands of children but also restaurants and inns, laundries, theater groups, sports clubs, sewing clubs, boys' clubs, girls' clubs, love affairs, trees and gardens, grass,

gates, gravestones, temples and shrines, family heirlooms, radios, classmates, books, courts of law, clothes, pets, groceries and markets, telephones, personal letters, automobiles, bicycles, horses—120 war horses—musical instruments, medicines and medical equipment, life savings, eye glasses, city records, sidewalks, family scrapbooks, monuments, engagements, marriages, employees, clocks and watches, public transportation, street signs, parents, [and] works of art.

"The whole of society," concluded the Japanese study, "was laid waste to its foundations."

A Hiroshima writer, Yōko Ōta, who survived the bombing recalled, "There was a fearful silence which made one feel that all people and all trees and vegetation were dead." An American psychiatrist, Robert Jay Lifton, who interviewed survivors at length wrote, "The inundation of death of the area closest to the hypocenter was such that if a man survived within 1,000 meters and was out of doors . . . more than nine-tenths of the people around him were fatalities."

Then there was the radiation sickness caused by direct radiation or radioactive fallout from the mushroom cloud. Some of those who did not die immediately seemed for a time to improve, but then, explains Lifton, they sickened:

Survivors began to notice in themselves and others a strange form of illness. It consisted of nausea, vomiting, and loss of appetite; diarrhea with large amounts of blood in the stools; fever and weakness; purple spots on various parts of the body from bleeding into the skin . . . inflammation and ulceration of the mouth, throat, and gums . . . bleeding from the mouth, gums, throat, rectum and urinary tract . . . loss of hair from the scalp and other parts of the body . . . extremely low white blood cell counts when these were taken . . . and in many cases a progressive course until death.

Earlier in the war, the population of Hiroshima had been near 400,000, but by August 6, 1945, the resident population numbered some 280,000 to 290,000 civilians and about 43,000 soldiers. More recent estimates of the number of Hiroshima residents killed by the atomic bomb are about 140,000, says Rhodes, but deaths from radiation-related illnesses continued, the five-year level reaching a total of 200,000 deaths by 1950. Rhodes indicates that a Yale Medical School pathologist, Averill A. Liebow, who worked in Hiroshima with a joint Japanese-American study group a few months after the war, computed that Little Boy produced casualties (including dead) 6,500 times more efficiently than an ordinary high-explosive bomb. Rhodes concludes his account of the attack on Hiroshima by quoting a young woman who was a fourth-grade student in Hiroshima at the time: "Those scientists who invented the . . . atomic bomb, what did they think would happen if they dropped it?"

This horrific incident described so well by Richard Rhodes, this unbelievable holocaust causing 200,000 deaths in a population of approximately 323,000, was caused by a small 12.5-kiloton atomic bomb of a design so simple that it did not need to be tested at full yield—a so-called gun bomb, where one piece of nuclear material is simply fired up the barrel of a small cannon to mate with a second piece fixed to the cannon's muzzle, forming a super-critical assembly and starting an explosive nuclear chain reaction.

Atomic bombs are charged with either of two heavy elements: highly enriched uranium (HEU) or a man-made element, plutonium, element 94. Natural uranium, element 92, is made up of two variant physical forms, called isotopes: 99.3 percent U-238 and 0.7 percent U-235. Both isotopes fission when bombarded with fast neutrons, but only U-235 chain-reacts. HEU is made from natural uranium by enriching its U-235 component to more than 80 percent.

U-238 also captures neutrons, another reason why most of it

has to be removed to make HEU suitable for atomic bombs. In a nuclear reactor, however, such capture can lead to the creation of the man-made element plutonium, which can then be chemically separated from its uranium matrix and used to charge an atomic bomb. Because plutonium tends to fission spontaneously, it is unsuitable for gun assembly; even if the pieces were fired together at 3,000 feet per second, they would melt down and fizzle before assembling. Since gun assemblies are inefficient for HEU and ineffective for plutonium, all modern nuclear weapons use an explosive assembly system called implosion, in which a shell of nuclear material is surrounded with shells of tamper metal and high explosives that explosively compress the nuclear material to a dense, supercritical mass so quickly that a chain reaction is triggered before there is time for predetonation. The tamped critical mass of HEU is about 15 kilograms; of plutonium, less than 5 kilograms. These small volumes of metal can destroy a city.

After atomic bombs were developed based on nuclear fission, they were adapted to serve as primers for another type of nuclear reaction, thermonuclear fusion. Atoms of light elements such as hydrogen can be induced to fuse together by compressing them while energizing them with extreme heat. When they fuse, some of their mass is converted into energy; atom for atom, fusion reactions release much more energy than fission reactions. In a hydrogen bomb, the initial compression and extreme heat—in the millions of degrees—is derived from a small but efficient fission "primary," about the size of a soccer ball, which channels enough energy to destroy a city around a fusion "secondary" no larger than a wastebasket, inducing fusion reactions in the secondary's hydrogen fuel. The upper limit on the size of a fission explosion is around 500 kilotons—half a megaton—because the developing chain reaction stops when the heating mass of uranium or plutonium expands beyond critical size. But because fusion requires no critical mass (so long as there is sufficient compression and heat, the hydrogen fuel will continue reacting), there is no theoretical upper limit to the yield of a thermonuclear weapon. The largest hydrogen bomb ever tested, by the Soviet Union, yielded more than 58 megatons, and the yield was deliberately scaled down from the weapon's designed yield of 150 megatons (by removing a U238 casing that would otherwise have fissioned and replacing it with lead) to spare the crew and the aircraft that dropped the bomb.

Hydrogen bombs are extremely complicated mechanisms, and no nation has developed them without extensive and easily detected weapon tests; the fission primary in particular, which has to deliver a powerful burst of radiation quickly, is a difficult scientific and engineering challenge. But a homemade gun device fueled with sufficient HEU would probably yield a Hiroshima-scale explosion or nearly so, and wrapping a subcritical mass of plutonium with plastic explosives might deliver a nuclear explosion in the range of hundreds of tons of TNT equivalent. These potentials emphasize the importance of guarding and controlling not only nuclear weapons but also stocks of uranium and plutonium.

So-called dirty bombs, in concept, are ordinary explosives attached to an industrial radioactive source containing such highly radioactive fission products as cobalt-60, iridium-192 or cesium-137, which are used for medical equipment sterilization, cancer treatment, and food irradiation. In theory, blowing up such a source could contaminate an area with radiation. In fact, only a relatively small area, perhaps the size of a city block, would be seriously contaminated, and the contaminated debris could be cleaned up by washing the area down; it would not, as some have speculated, "remain uninhabitable for years." Hiroshima and Nagasaki, for example, are both thriving cities today, and the towns around the Chernobyl nuclear power plant accident are recovering. The real impact of a dirty bomb would be psychological, inducing fear and possible panic.

With the development and deployment of long-range ballistic missiles beginning in the late 1950s, it became possible to deliver advanced nuclear weapons intercontinentally, from the Soviet Union to the United States and vice versa, within thirty minutes and with ever-increasing accuracy. The M-X or Peacekeeper intercontinental ballistic missile type deployed by the United States in the 1980s had a CEP of .1 miles. CEP (circular error probable) is a standard for measuring missile accuracy. In the case of the M-X, it meant that half of the ten nuclear warheads carried by the missile could be expected to fall within a .1 mile radius of the target—about 500 feet (as it was once explained to me, that means that five of the ten warheads of an M-X missile launched from the Kwajalein atoll in the Pacific Ocean could be made to fall within the courtyard of the Pentagon). And each of those warheads had a 500-kiloton explosive yield, about thirty-five times more power than the Hiroshima bomb. Many thousands of intercontinental ballistic missiles with nuclear warheads remain in place today, more than ten years after the end of the Cold War, on hair-trigger alert, ready to cause unimaginable destruction; there is little prospect that this will change in the near future. This situation represents an almost unbelievable hostage to fortune.

If thermonuclear war had occurred between the United States and the Soviet Union during the Cold War, civilization would likely have been destroyed. This nearly did happen during the Cuban Missile Crisis. In October 1962, President John F. Kennedy was assured by the CIA and the joint chiefs of staff that none of the Soviet nuclear weapon missile systems situated in Cuba were yet operational, and that it would therefore be safe for the United States to invade Cuba in order to remove this growing threat. The president was strongly urged to do so by the joint chiefs of staff and the Congress. Nevertheless, Kennedy chose to settle the crisis peaceably. Years later, it was discovered that about 150 Soviet short-range nuclear missile systems in Cuba had been operational and the release order had been given in Moscow should Cuba be invaded by the United States. Had Kennedy agreed to invade, Miami would have been destroyed and there would have been a very great risk of escalation to all-out nuclear war. This was not the only close call during the forty-five years of the Cold War.

The Cold War has now passed into history. The Berlin Wall fell and the division of Europe into enormous hostile camps ended between 1989 and 1990. The Soviet Union dissolved on Christmas Day, 1991. More than ten years after the end of the Cold War, there remain many thousands of nuclear weapons in the possession of Russia and the United States. Given that the Cold War nuclear confrontation has now ended, these weapons have little purpose, and do not add to the security of the countries that possess them. Arguably, the large numbers of weapons in the possession of the United States and Russia might, by their very existence, be as much of a danger to the countries that possess them as to anyone else. Today, the threat is that unstable countries (called "rogue" states) or terrorist organizations might acquire nuclear weapons and use them.

Considering what happened at Hiroshima on August 6, 1945, and at Nagasaki three days later, can the use of these weapons, which incinerate human beings, poison atmospheres, crush buildings, and destroy cities ever be justified? In the dangerous nuclear arms race that accompanied the Cold War, large numbers of nuclear weapons were used for "nuclear deterrence," discouraging the Soviet Union from using or threatening to use its nuclear weapons against the United States, and vice versa. Nuclear deterrence brought stability between the two superpower antagonists. But what role do these weapons have now? Even if there were some conceivable battlefield or other active military role for nuclear weapons, the United States should be extremely reluctant to ever again consider their use. The only practical role for nuclear weapons now is as a limited deterrent in relatively small numbers and as a hedge against unforeseen developments until some sort of truly reliable worldwide inspection regime and means of enforcement can be established—probably years into the future.

3

An Overview of
International Law and
Arms Control

IN THE END, IT IS THE RULE OF LAW THAT DIS-
tinguishes civilization from barbarism. It has taken thousands
of years for humankind to develop into a community of civilized
states, the majority of which are governed by law. Governments
were formed in ancient times to provide security and an opportunity for economic development. Gradually the concept of the
supremacy of law over the government and society began to prevail; only slowly did the king accept that he too was subject to
the law.

Approximately 400 years ago, efforts began to bring the rule
of law to interstate relations as well in order to promote a system
of international order. Since the Age of Enlightenment in the
eighteenth century, the world community has accepted this idea
that governments must be subject to the rule of law in order to
be considered legitimate. Agreements between states exist today

that affect much of the life of the world community. Commercial agreements such as the International Telecommunications Union and the World Trade Organization help to support the economic life of our planet.

Many of these commercial treaties (as well as some human rights accords and agreements on the environment) have operated successfully for decades, but bringing law to the field of international security has proven to be far more difficult. There have been a number of attempts over the last two centuries. Today, most prominently, the Charter of the United Nations, adopted in 1945 after World War II (in which sixty million people died) attempted to establish a framework for order in a chaotic world. Pursuant to the principles of the charter, there have been treaties negotiated to limit armaments as well as to establish rules of international humanitarian law. The Nuclear Non-Proliferation Treaty is the most important of the treaties limiting armaments, and, in addition to the United Nations Charter, is the bedrock upon which international security is built today. Rules of warfare have been developed, such as the Geneva Protocol of 1925 that prohibits the use in war of chemical and biological weapons, as well as so-called customary rules of international law (rules generally recognized by international tribunals due to their widespread and long-standing acceptance by the world community), for example, the rule of proportionality, which provides that in warfare it is contrary to law to respond to an armed attack with significantly greater force than is necessary to repel and defeat the attacker.

Some have argued in recent years that with the end of the Cold War, the subsequent increase in worldwide disorder, and the growing threat of international terrorism, treaties limiting armaments, rules of warfare, and international humanitarian law are all becoming obsolete. Such commentators imply that we will have to return to the code of the jungle to deal with the current situation. Indeed, some have argued that treaties controlling armaments are only suitable in times of peace (when they are irrelevant) and that the gloves must be taken off in times of confrontation and terrorism.

But what kind of world do we want to live in? Order imposed by force may be effective in the short term, but long-term security and peace in today's world, as in the past, require rules that nations respect and cooperation among states of the world community. World order imposed exclusively by force has not succeeded in the last 400 years, as the many attempts at hegemony resulting in destructive conflicts has demonstrated, and it is unlikely to succeed now. World order can be effectively achieved only by the consent of the world community based on an accepted system of treaties and rules. For example, from the Peace of Westphalia in 1648 until the wars of the French Revolution beginning in 1795, there were no wars that could be considered total wars such as the Wars of Religion that decimated Europe in the first half of the seventeenth century, because warfare had strict limits that all of the great world powers understood and respected. Similar limits were placed on warfare in Europe between the final defeat of Napoleon and World War I by balance-of-power diplomacy.

In the 1960s, there was a recognized threat that nuclear weapons might spread around the world, creating many nuclear armed states, thereby ensuring that Yugoslavia would have had such weapons at the time of the Balkan Wars, that Iraq would have had them before Desert Storm, and that states such as Syria, Libya, Iran, Nigeria, and North Korea would have them today. Indeed, many countries—and, possibly, international terrorist organizations—might have had them today if not for the NPT and the international rule of behavior it established. Are we to assume that this rule is no longer relevant? That it and similar rules regulating armaments should be allowed to simply wither away, and that U.S. armed forces should establish and maintain the peace everywhere and indefinitely? It would take a very large army to even attempt to do this.

The international treaties on arms control and nonproliferation that have helped to keep the peace and reduce the risk of war for the past fifty years essentially follow three tracks: First, there are multilateral treaties that prohibit nuclear weapons in environments where they have not yet appeared, limit nuclear weapons generally, and prohibit chemical and biological weapons. A multilateral treaty involves three or more parties (often a very large number) and is usually negotiated at a special conference called for that purpose or at an organization of the United Nations. Consensus rule is normally applied, meaning that all countries in the negotiation must agree to the entire treaty—at least, none must overtly object to anything in it—before the negotiation can be brought to a successful close. Second, there are bilateral treaties between the United States and the Soviet Union (and later Russia), limiting strategic and medium-range nuclear-weapon delivery vehicles (missiles and bombers). Bilateral treaties between two countries are sometimes negotiated at a neutral site, and sometimes at one capitol or alternating between capitols. Both parties, of course, have to agree to the treaty in its entirety before the negotiation is successfully completed. And third, there is a series of treaties limiting conventional weapons of an especially injurious nature worldwide and major conventional weapon systems regionally.

Normally, at the end of a negotiation, a country signs a treaty. But it is not subject to the obligations of that treaty—it is not a party—until it ratifies the treaty. Ratification is by the head of the government of a country, usually after approval of that country's national legislature—in the case of the United States, the Senate. Treaties only enter into force (or become effective) after both countries (in the case of a bilateral treaty), or a specified number of countries (in the case of a multilateral treaty), have ratified it. Under the Vienna Convention on the Law of Treaties, considered part of international law, upon signature of a treaty, a state is obligated not to defeat the object and purpose of a treaty (that is, to do something to make the system to be established by the treaty impossible)—for example, by conducting nuclear tests after signing a treaty banning such tests. This obligation lasts until ratification by the state and entry into force of the treaty, at which time the provisions of the treaty apply, or, alternatively, until the state formally declares it will not ratify.

Lower-level international agreements, sometimes called "executive agreements," can establish international legal commitments, and enter into force upon signature. They are often subsidiary agreements implementing treaties, but, unlike treaties, whose ratification creates domestic law indistinguishable in a legal sense from legislation passed by a national legislature, executive agreements do not create domestic law and are only binding internationally. Often, but not always, they are not subject to a ratification process. Other international agreements are considered to create politically, not legally, binding arrangements. Since there are no legal obligations, ratification is unnecessary; these agreements come into force upon signature. Whenever a state takes action relying on the commitments in politically binding undertakings, it raises the status of those commitments and they can acquire near-legal force. For example, in 1996 the International Court of Justice (the World Court) indicated that the security assurances given by the NPT nuclear weapon states not to attack the NPT nonnuclear states with nuclear weapons should be considered as legally binding as similar commitments contained in protocols to nuclear-weapon-free zone treaties, which are legally binding.

With the advent of the nuclear age in 1945, various concepts were explored to try to limit the spread of nuclear weapons and the threat they pose to humanity, beginning with the Baruch Plan in 1946. But, with the explosion of the first Soviet atomic bomb in 1949, the nuclear arms race was on in earnest. Britain followed suit in 1952, France in 1960, and China in 1964. The United States and the Soviet Union began testing thermonuclear weapons (hydrogen bombs) in the 1950s. In 1958, the then three nuclear weapon states (the United States, Britain, and the Soviet Union) agreed to a moratorium on nuclear explosive testing. This halt in nuclear weapon testing lasted for three years, but collapsed in 1961 when the Soviet Union initiated a series of nuclear weapon tests with the largest nuclear explosion of all time: 58 megatons.

The first practical attempts to limit nuclear weapons began of necessity in the late 1950s with the idea that nuclear weapons could be prohibited from spreading to environments where they had not yet appeared. The first modern arms control treaty, the Antarctic Treaty, was signed in 1959 and entered into force in 1961. Among other things, it prohibited the testing of nuclear weapons or the conduct of any measures of a military nature in Antarctica, thereby in effect making Antarctica the first nuclear-weapon-free area. This treaty and similar treaties that followed were based on the premise that it is easier to exclude armaments from an area than to eliminate them once they have been introduced. As the first modern arms control treaty involving many nations and directly affecting nuclear weapons, the Antarctic Treaty served as a model for later "nonarmament" treaties.

The next treaty of this type was the Outer Space Treaty of 1967. It prohibited placing nuclear weapons or any other weapons of mass destruction (chemical or biological) in orbit or stationing them anywhere else in outer space. It also banned the establishment of military facilities on any heavenly body, such as the moon, and provided that outer space should be used exclusively for peaceful purposes. This treaty and its provisions are at the center of the current debate over whether outer space should be weaponized (with defensive and perhaps offensive weapons deployed for the first time) or only militarized (with military reconnaissance and navigation satellites and similar vehicles, which have long been present and are not prohibited by the treaty, deployed, as is the case now).

The Seabed Arms Control Treaty of 1972 prohibited the placing of nuclear weapons or other weapons of mass destruction on the beds of the high seas, and numerous nuclear-weapon-free zone treaties prohibit nuclear weapons in the territories that they cover. Nuclear weapons cannot be developed, placed, or tested in the areas covered by these treaties, although transit through the areas by ships and planes which may be carrying nuclear weapons is allowed. The nuclear-weapon-free zone treaties (and the areas they cover) include the 1967 Treaty of Tlatelolco (Latin America and the Caribbean); the 1986 Treaty of Rarotonga (South Pacific); the 1995 Treaty of Bangkok (Southeast Asia); and the 1996 Treaty of Pelindaba (Africa). As a result of these treaties, the entire land area of the Southern Hemisphere and some land areas of the Northern Hemisphere are off-limits to nuclear weapons. In 2000 Mongolia declared itself to be a one-state nuclear-weapon-free zone, and for some years, Kazakhstan, Kyrgyzstan, Tajikistan, Turkmenistan, and Uzbekistan have been negotiating to establish a nuclear-weapon-free zone for Central Asia. Thus, large areas of the earth and outer space have become nuclear-weapon-free zones.

The Antarctic Treaty and the Outer Space Treaty were forerunners to the most important international security treaty of them all, the 1968 Nuclear Non-Proliferation Treaty, the foundation on which a large part of the existing international arms limitation measures are based. In a sense, the philosophy of the Antarctic Treaty was followed here as well. The NPT was drafted to halt nuclear proliferation where it was in 1968. No additional states would be allowed to acquire nuclear weapons, and those five states that possessed nuclear weapons at that time were allowed to keep them, under certain conditions. Foremost among the conditions was that when the nuclear weapon states joined the NPT, they accepted an obligation to pursue nuclear disarmament measures with the ultimate objective of the complete elimination of nuclear weapons, and to share peaceful nuclear technology. The authority of the five nuclear weapon states to possess nuclear weapons under the NPT is intended to be temporary, not permanent. The commitment of the rest of the members of this treaty, the non-nuclear weapon states (now 182 nations—most of the world) not to have nuclear weapons is permanent.

First among the nuclear-disarmament measures intended as a step toward the eventual abolition of nuclear weapons was a complete or comprehensive ban on explosive nuclear weapon tests. The effort to stop nuclear weapon testing goes far back in the history of the nuclear age. The first efforts to negotiate an international agreement ending nuclear tests began in 1955. Several events had raised concerns in the international community over weapon testing. In 1954, a U.S. hydrogen bomb test had delivered a much greater explosion than expected, and a Japanese fishing vessel hundreds of miles away had been contaminated by radioactive fallout. In another incident that took place near the same time, rain containing radioactive debris from a Soviet hydrogen bomb test fell on Japan. And there were indications that radioactive byproducts of nuclear explosions were entering and poisoning the food chain—particularly strontium 90 in milk.

After the collapse of the nuclear-testing moratorium in 1961, the United States and the Soviet Union renewed their efforts to achieve a treaty prohibiting nuclear weapon tests, but there were still differences between the Soviet Union and the West on how to verify a ban on nuclear testing, particularly on underground tests. The United States pressed hard for an agreement on testing, but verification proved a problem. The United States wanted both on-site inspection as well as unmanned seismic stations on Soviet territory so it could be sure to be able to detect any underground nuclear weapon test conducted by the Soviet Union in secret. After months of negotiation, the Soviets agreed in principle to both, but the two sides could not get together on the number of on-site inspections that would be allowed per year or the number of unmanned seismic stations that would be allowed on each territory. To break this impasse, in June 1963, President John F. Kennedy proposed to negotiate a treaty with the Soviet Union and Britain prohibiting nuclear weapons tests in the atmosphere, outer space, and underwater in the ocean—everywhere except underground. This measure would solve the environmental concerns with nuclear weapon testing and it would be verifiable.

The result was the Limited Test Ban Treaty of 1963, which prohibited nuclear weapon test explosions in the atmosphere, under water, and in outer space. It also banned underground nuclear explosions if radioactive debris from such an explosion would cross national borders. Following the signing of this treaty, nuclear tests actually increased in number after they went underground. The Limited Test Ban Treaty, which eventually had 110 parties, did not address the arms control concerns of the nonnuclear weapon states, who wanted a halt in the development of nuclear weapons in exchange for their agreement not to have them. The nonnuclear weapon states pressed for a complete or comprehensive ban on nuclear weapon tests. It was many years before the LTBT pledge to seek a treaty establishing a comprehensive ban on nuclear tests (covering all environments—including underground) was realized. When the NPT parties agreed to make the NPT permanent in 1995, the nonnuclear weapon states extracted a written commitment from the nuclear weapon states to achieve a comprehensive nuclear test ban treaty by 1996.

The Comprehensive Nuclear-Test-Ban Treaty (CTBT) was signed in 1996, establishing a complete and worldwide ban on all nuclear test explosions and providing for a vast international monitoring system. Some one hundred and fourteen countries have ratified the treaty. The U.S. Senate rejected the CTBT in 1999 and it has not yet come into force because a number of necessary parties have not yet joined.

Another important area of multilateral arms control has been the long effort to ban chemical and biological weapons from the arsenals of states. The 1925 Geneva Protocol prohibited the use in war of chemical (poison gas) and biological weapons. However, reservations (legal conditions put by a state on its obligations under a treaty that it is joining) taken by states when they joined the protocol effectively converted it into an agreement banning the first use in war of these weapons. But the right to retaliate in kind was preserved, and the protocol failed to address chemical and biological weapon arsenals.

The bilateral arms control process between the United States and the Soviet Union (later Russia) began in the 1960s with the objective of ending the nuclear arms race, establishing strategic stability, and reducing the risk of nuclear war, as well as contributing to the implementation of the arms control obligations of the two countries under the NPT. President Lyndon B. Johnson had agreed with the Soviet leadership to begin the bilateral strategic arms negotiations in 1968, but the Soviet invasion of Czechoslovakia forced a postponement. In November 1969 the Strategic Arms Limitation Talks (SALT) began under President Richard Nixon. The first phase of SALT, called the SALT I negotiations, lasted until May 1972. The result of these negotiations was an interim agreement on strategic arms that was essentially a freeze of the long-range nuclear missile forces (ranges over 3,000 miles, considered to be strategic weapons) of the United States and the Soviet Union as they stood in May 1972. Under the Interim Agreement, the United States was permitted about 1,700 strategic nuclear missiles, both land- and sea-based. The Soviet Union was permitted about 2,550. The United States believed it could tolerate the disparity for the five-year term of the agreement because its missiles had multiple warheads; in 1972 the Soviets had not yet developed this technology, known as multiple independently targetable reentry vehicles (MIRVs), which enabled a single missile to attack many targets. Also, the Interim Agreement did not cover strategic bombers, in which the United States had a significant advantage.

In May 1972 a treaty restricting strategic defense to very low levels, called the Anti-Ballistic Missile (ABM) Treaty was also signed, limiting the deployment in the field of missile defense systems to two sites each for the United States and the Soviet Union. As a result of an amendment to the ABM Treaty in 1974, this limit was reduced to one site per side, thus reducing strategic missile defense to a level just above extinction. The theory behind the ABM Treaty was that if one side built strategic defense, the other side would simply add more offense to compensate; therefore, limiting strategic defense to a low level was stabilizing. Also, in 1972 it was believed that if one side were to build a missile defense system, the other side might be led to believe that the first side was pursuing a first-strike capability, and that the missile defense was intended to ward off a retaliatory response. Such a situation could make nuclear war more likely in a crisis; as a result, limiting strategic defense could reduce the danger of war. The ABM Treaty entered into force in 1972; however, after a long internal debate, the United States withdrew from the treaty in accordance with its terms in June 2002.

Negotiations began in 1973 to conclude a permanent treaty limiting strategic offensive forces to succeed the Interim Agreement upon its expiration in 1977. The negotiations, called the SALT II negotiations, were not in fact completed until 1979, and thus the Interim Agreement was informally extended in 1977. The Soviets had begun putting MIRV warheads on their strategic missiles in 1975, which made the Interim Agreement balance untenable and caused the strategic arms limitation process to be more politically controversial in the 1970s.

In 1979, the United States and the Soviet Union signed the SALT II Treaty, a comprehensive agreement limiting strategic offense. It placed a limit of 2,400 on the long-range nuclear missiles, both land- and sea-based, as well as the strategic bombers of each party. It also had a number of sub-limits for missiles with MIRV warheads, along with limits on new systems. It effectively capped the strategic arms race; for the first time, the vast nuclear deployments of the United States and the Soviet Union, which could obliterate them both and the entire world in a matter of minutes began to be brought under control. Like the SALT I agreements, the ABM Treaty, and the Interim Agreement, the SALT II Treaty was to be verified by "national technical means," a widely understood cover name for spy satellites, which were thereby legitimized by these agreements. By its terms, the treaty was to last until December 31, 1985, but it was never ratified by the United States, due to the political controversy that had enveloped the treaty as a result of the 1980 U.S. presidential election. However, along with the Interim Agreement, SALT II was informally observed by the two parties until 1986, when the United States withdrew from this arrangement.

In 1981, the Reagan administration reformed the strategic arms negotiating process into the Strategic Arms Reduction Talks, or START. It also began negotiations with the Soviet Union to limit the two parties' medium-range nuclear missiles in Europe (and eventually worldwide). These negotiations were known as the Intermediate-Range Nuclear Forces (INF) negotiations. Little progress was realized in either of these negotiations in the first half of the 1980s, but the negotiations were recast in 1985 as a three-part negotiation called the Nuclear and Space Arms Negotiations—consisting of the ongoing INF and START negotiations, and the negotiation on space arms insisted upon by the Soviet Union as a result of the commencement of the U.S. Strategic Defense Initiative (SDI, sometimes referred to as "Star Wars") space-based missile defense program. The space arms negotiations never got off the ground, but by 1988, SDI, potentially in conflict with the ABM Treaty, was fading away. The INF negotiations, on other hand, were successfully completed in 1987. The Intermediate-Range Nuclear Forces Treaty was signed by Presidents Ronald Reagan and Mikhail Gorbachev in December 1987, and entered into force in June 1988. It successfully eliminated the two countries' medium-range nuclear missiles (with ranges of 200–3,000 miles) on a worldwide basis. It also contained, for the first time in any agreement limiting nuclear weapons, a broad and intrusive on-site inspection regime in addition to verification by "national technical means." In this, it set the pattern for the future.

Meanwhile, the START negotiations ground on to a conclusion. In July 1991, Presidents George H. W. Bush and Gorbachev signed the START I Treaty, just months before the dissolution of the Soviet Union. Because the dissolution of the Soviet Union left strategic offensive nuclear arms on the territories of Ukraine, Belarus, and Kazakhstan, as well as Russia, a follow-on agreement was concluded in 1992 (known as the Lisbon Protocol because of where it was signed), substituting Russia, Ukraine, Belarus, and Kazakhstan as parties to the START I Treaty in place of the Soviet Union. The START I Treaty reduced strategic offensive forces to 6,000 strategic nuclear warheads for the United States (actually 7,500, because of a special exclusion for certain bomber weapons), 6,000 for Russia, and, by means of the Lisbon Protocol, zero for Ukraine, Belarus, and Kazakhstan, who joined the NPT as nonnuclear states. The unit of account stated in the treaty is strategic nuclear warheads instead of strategic missiles and bombers, as in the SALT agreements, but because of the way they are counted, the result is the same. The START I Treaty was a truly comprehensive agreement, hundreds of pages long, which provided for complete limitations on strategic offensive nuclear weapons. It reduced strategic nuclear forces by 50 percent, and, like the INF Treaty, had a complicated and intrusive on-site inspection regime to supplement the spy satellites. It entered into force in 1994 and contained a seven-year period for the reductions to be accomplished. In 2001, the United States and Russia announced that the required reductions had been completed.

Shortly after the signing of the START I Treaty, Presidents Bush and Boris Yeltsin agreed in principle to a START II Treaty, built upon the START I Treaty regime, which reduced strategic weapons even further, to 3,000 to 3,500 for each side. The START II Treaty was signed by the two presidents in January 1993. In 1997, Presidents William J. Clinton and Yeltsin agreed in principle to a third reduction, to 2,000 to 2,500 strategic weapons apiece, but this understanding was never converted into a START III Treaty. The START II Treaty never came into force. It was approved by the U.S. Senate and ratified by the United States in 1994, but Russia was concerned about some of the deadlines. In 1997 the dates were modified at the same START III meeting between Presidents Clinton and Yeltsin, and Russia ratified the treaty but withdrew its ratification in 2000 after the U.S. ABM Treaty withdrawal. The debate over missile defense in the United States had become so intense that it was not possible to achieve U.S. Senate approval and ratification of the revised START II Treaty by the end of 2000. In 2002, the United States abandoned the START process.

In June 2002, the United States and Russia signed a brief, new type of strategic arms limitation treaty called the Strategic Offensive Reductions Treaty (SORT), which provides that by the last day of 2012, the United States and Russia will reduce the operational strategic weapons that each has in the field on alert to 1,700 to 2,200. It is presumed that those weapons removed will not be eliminated but rather placed in ready reserve or storage.

In the late 1960s, efforts began to negotiate international agreements to eliminate stocks of chemical and biological weapons. Chemical weapons proved too difficult to address at the time, because they existed in states' arsenals and had been used in war in the recent past. But in 1972 an agreement was concluded, called the Biological Weapons Convention, which prohibited parties from acquiring biological weapons "in any circumstances," even for retaliation. The convention also mandated the destruction of existing stockpiles of biological weapons. Although the convention currently has over 100 parties, it has only very limited verification provisions, and efforts to develop a subsequent verification protocol have not been successful.

After many years of discussion, a companion agreement limiting chemical weapons was finally agreed upon and signed in 1993. The Chemical Weapons Convention, with nearly 150 parties, prohibits the acquisition of chemical weapons "in any circumstances" and provides for the destruction of existing stocks, as does the Biological Weapons Convention. However, it differs from that agreement in that it has an elaborate verification system, which includes regulated on-site inspection.

In modern times a series of arms control agreements has focused on conventional weapons (largely those in Europe), but with an important and ongoing subtext of attempted worldwide limitation on conventional weapons of an especially injurious or destructive nature. This began with the "confidence-building measures" contained in the 1975 Final Act of the Conference on Security and Cooperation in Europe, known as the Helsinki Final Act. Among many other provisions dealing with the sanctity of international borders and human rights in Europe, the Helsinki Final Act provided for prior notification of military exercises involving more than 25,000 troops, and exchanges of observers during such maneuvers. This led to a series of conferences and agreements vastly expanding the confidence-building-measure regime, thereby providing for an abundance of exchanges of observers, notifications, and information, which greatly helped to stabilize the political and military situation in Europe. Prominent among these are the concluding document of the Stockholm Conference of 1986 and the four Vienna documents on confidence-building measures of 1990, 1992, 1994, and 1999.

As part of the ongoing process set in motion by the Helsinki Final Act, generally referred to as the Helsinki Process, negotiations began in 1987 to limit conventional armaments in Europe. First, there were the mandate talks, which lasted from 1987 to 1989, to set the framework for negotiations. The negotiations on conventional armed forces in Europe, known as the CFE negotiations, began in 1989 and were completed in 1990. The CFE negotiations ended with the signing of the CFE Treaty in November 1990 at a ceremony in Paris involving all the members of the NATO alliance and the former Warsaw Pact alliance (except for East Germany, which merged with West Germany in 1990 after the fall of the Berlin Wall), the two armed camps which had formerly divided Europe. The CFE Treaty limited the major components of combined arms in Europe (measured from the Atlantic Ocean to the Ural Mountains in Russia), i.e., battle tanks, artillery, armored combat vehicles, combat aircraft, and attack helicopters. It provided for equality between East and West, and security for all parties. The negotiations were very much led by the United States and assisted by NATO Allies, pulling a reluctant Soviet Union and the other Eastern states along. The CFE Treaty is generally regarded as the treaty that ended the Cold War, and will be the basis of security in Europe for decades to come.

The effort to limit conventional arms has taken on increasing importance with the end of the Cold War in 1991. The international agreement known as the Convention on Certain Conventional Weapons (CCW) was negotiated in the 1970s and signed in 1981. It entered into force in 1983. It is essentially a framework with several protocols, each of which limits a particular type of conventional weapon on a worldwide basis. A party to the CCW may sign one or more of the protocols, which are separate agreements. Protocol 1 prohibits fragmentation weapons (weapons that create fragments in the bodies of their victims). Protocol 2 places some limits on the use of land mines and booby traps. It was amended at the Review Conference in 1996, but an attempt to convert it into a complete ban on antipersonnel land mines failed. This failure gave rise to the process which led to the negotiation of the 1997 Ottawa Convention, which prohibited antipersonnel land mines. Protocol 3 prohibits the use of incendiary weapons against civilian populations. Protocol 4 bans laser weapons, which cause permanent blindness.

With the end of the Cold War, emplaced antipersonnel land mines pose an increasing serious threat to humanity. There are an estimated 100 million land mines still in the ground around the world, many of them at unrecorded locations. Approximately 25,000 innocent civilians are killed each year as a result of encountering one of these land mines. A series of diplomatic meetings took place in 1997 in Vienna, Brussels, and Oslo concerning the prohibition of antipersonnel land mines. At the Oslo meeting, the draft treaty prohibiting antipersonnel land mines, known as the Ottawa Convention, was approved. The convention was opened for signature in Ottawa in December 1997, and entered into force on March 1, 1999, upon the ratification of the convention by the fortieth state. At the Oslo negotiations, the United States attempted to gain exemptions for antipersonnel land mines in South Korea as well as antipersonnel land mines deployed to protect anti-tank mines. Failing to achieve these exemptions, the United States declined to sign the convention. China and Russia have also not signed.

The global diffusion of small arms, when considered as a whole, is also a serious threat to all countries. Small arms, in this text, means weapons such as machine guns, grenade launchers, and automatic rifles. The international community is gradually attempting to come to grips with this problem, energized by the fact that these weapons are continually being used to destabilize governments, particularly in Africa and Latin America. Some initial steps have been taken to control illegal international transfers of these weapons, but much work remains to be done.

International humanitarian law applicable to armed conflict, built up over several centuries, is also important. In its July 8, 1996, *Advisory Opinion on the Legality of the Threat or Use of Nuclear Weapons* (mentioned above in the reference to negative security assurances), the International Court of Justice set forth the essence of these rules in paragraph 78. "The cardinal principles contained in the texts constituting the fabric of humanitarian law are the following: The first is aimed at the protection of the civilian population and civilian objects and establishes the distinction between combatants and noncombatants; states must never make civilians the object of attack and must consequently never use weapons that are incapable of distinguishing between civilian and military targets. According to the second principle, it is prohibited to cause unnecessary suffering to combatants. It is accordingly prohibited to use weapons causing them such harm or uselessly aggravating their suffering. In application of that second principle, states do not have unlimited freedom of choice of means in the weapons they use." All of the major states of the world accept these principles, including the United States. These principles and their elaboration in treaties and rules of international law are the basis for our condemnation of international crimes such as those committed by the Milosevic regime in Yugoslavia, the Saddam Hussein regime in Iraq, the Hutu regime in Rwanda, and many others. The World Court recognized in its opinion that these rules of law and the international treaties limiting armaments and establishing specific rules of warfare are all part of one fabric and have as their objective a more secure, stable, and peaceful world.

But these rules and treaties cannot be sustained without effort. Some states ignore their own obligations when this is convenient; others cheat on their obligations; some do not see the benefit to them of observing the rules if others do not; and some reject their obligations outright. These are always problems in establishing the rule of law in individual nations and the international community. It is for those states that truly seek a peaceful world order based on law and security to observe their own obligations and join together to enforce them against those states that reject them.

The trend today is not positive, however. On February 11, 2003, before the Senate Select Committee on Intelligence, U.S. Central Intelligence Agency Director George Tenet described a "continued weakening of the international non-proliferation consensus" and asserted that "the domino theory of the twenty-first century may well be nuclear," as President John F. Kennedy had feared in the 1960s, before the negotiation of the NPT (*National Journal*, July 12, 2003, p. 2268).

When Mikhail Gorbachev, the last president of the Soviet Union, was in office, he used to express the hope that the Soviet Union would become a "law-based state." President Vladimir Putin has explicitly recognized this objective as highly important to Russia, even though it is of necessity a long road from a totalitarian dictatorship to a state ruled by law. Many other governments of emerging states in the latter part of the twentieth century have acknowledged the centrality of this goal. In the

United States, law students are taught that the legal process is fragile and that it is the duty of the lawyer to protect it. The same is true of the emerging worldwide consensus that in seeking security, states must be governed by rules of conduct. These rules apply to the weapons arsenals they employ, their actions during warfare, and the decision to use armed force. It is in the interest of all to preserve and strengthen this worldwide consensus at all costs. It is the only effective long-term response to barbarism and disorder.

4

The Cornerstone
of Security: The Nuclear
Non-Proliferation Treaty

IN A *FOREIGN AFFAIRS* ARTICLE SEVERAL YEARS ago, Jonathan Schell argued that the solutions to some political problems lie "outside the bounds of contemporary political acceptability"; that sometimes the right approach seems politically untenable, and, as a result, we choose instead an ostensibly more attractive middle course ("The Folly of Arms Control," September–October 2000). But the politically easy answer may carry unspeakably dangerous consequences. According to Schell, such was the case when the Allies chose to appease Nazi Germany rather than resolutely oppose Hitler's aggression, or when the United States, refusing to choose between full occupation of and full withdrawal from Vietnam, chose instead a path that led to gradual escalation of the war, with disastrous consequences.

Schell argued that we are at another such juncture today: The human race has reached the point where (under U.S. leadership) it must choose between a world free of nuclear weapons and a widely proliferated world. He suggests that the prevailing notion of making every effort to stop the spread of nuclear weapons while holding on to a large nuclear stockpile ourselves is inherently contradictory. Somehow that contradiction must be addressed. Schell stated that there is no middle road here: If we are to prevent the spread of nuclear weapons, we must be prepared to eventually give up our own weapons. If we cannot give up our own weapons, then we must be prepared to live in a world in which every nation that can acquire nuclear weapons does so.

I would not go so far as to say that we must choose between complete nuclear disarmament and the rampant spread of nuclear weapons, but I do agree with Schell's premise that we are at a crucial juncture in the world's relationship with nuclear weapons. Our approach to nuclear arms control and nonproliferation in recent years has drifted so far away from the commitments we have made that we are now approaching a point where we may have to make a conscious choice: Do we accept a widely proliferated world in which thirty or more nations have nuclear weapons and begin to develop plans to try to manage that world, or do we pursue a strong, vigorous, effective nuclear nonproliferation regime?

There can be no underestimating the importance of this decision. The principal threats to U.S. security today center not on the risks posed by powerful nation states but on the weakness of states such as Russia (which may be potentially unable to prevent part of its vast stockpile of nuclear weapons, nuclear explosive material, and other threatening technologies and scientific weapon expertise left over from the Cold War from proliferating into dangerous hands) and on transnational concerns such as terrorism, economic instability, wide-scale poverty and disease, and environmental degradation, all of which reinforce the central threat to our security: the spread of nuclear weapons to unstable countries, terrorist organizations, religious cults, and the like.

For more than thirty years, the Nuclear Non-Proliferation

Treaty has been a firm bulwark against this threat. Because of the NPT, the international community has thus far been largely successful in preventing the spread of nuclear weapons. The predictions made during the Kennedy administration that as many as twenty-five to thirty nations would have nuclear weapons integrated into their arsenals by the end of the 1970s did not come true, thanks to the NPT. The International Atomic Energy Agency reports that, while many nations now possess the technological capabilities to produce nuclear weapons, only a handful have crossed the nuclear threshold. In 2000, then U.S. Secretary of State Madeleine Albright referred to the NPT as "the most important multilateral arms control agreement in history."

The success of the NPT is no accident. It is rooted in a carefully crafted central bargain often referred to as the NPT "basic bargain": In exchange for a commitment from the nonnuclear weapon states (today, some 182 nations) not to develop or otherwise acquire nuclear weapons and to submit to international safeguards intended to verify compliance with the commitment (Article 2), the NPT nuclear weapon states promised unfettered access to peaceful nuclear technologies (e.g., nuclear power reactors and nuclear medicine; Article 4), and pledged to engage in disarmament negotiations aimed at the ultimate elimination of their nuclear arsenals (Article 6). It is this basic bargain that for the last three decades has formed the central underpinnings of U.S. nuclear nonproliferation strategy.

When the NPT was negotiated in 1968, three of the seventeen negotiating parties—Germany, Italy, and Sweden—were unwilling to give the NPT permanent status. They were uncertain whether it would be successful, and were concerned about the economic effect of the treaty safeguards on their domestic nuclear industries. And perhaps they were unwilling to permanently forswear nuclear weapons at that time. Thus, the NPT was given a twenty-five-year life span, at the end of which the treaty parties would have the option, by majority vote, to extend the treaty indefinitely, extend it for a fixed period after which it would expire, or extend it for a series of fixed periods (which could lead to periodic crises for the treaty and its eventual termination). Despite the treaty's success in stemming proliferation, when the international community met to review the treaty and decide on its duration in 1995 at the Review and Extension Conference, a significant number of key nonnuclear weapon states were dissatisfied with the progress made by the nuclear weapon states in fulfilling their side of the bargain. As a result, many were reluctant to accept a permanent NPT that would lock them into what they saw as an inherently discriminatory regime. While the NPT does not explicitly legitimize the arsenals of the nuclear weapon states, many NPT nonnuclear parties have political reasons for wanting to see equality among all states in terms of nuclear weapons, and indeed a system cannot forever survive in which some states are considered superior to others because they are allowed to have nuclear weapons. Many non-Western states were concerned that a permanent NPT would remove the incentive for the nuclear powers to reduce their arsenals.

In order to address this concern, the NPT state parties at the extension conference negotiated an associated consensus agreement, called the Statement of Principles and Objectives for Nuclear Nonproliferation and Disarmament, intended to strengthen the regime and, politically if not legally, condition the extension of the treaty. Because the treaty parties did not want to jeopardize the treaty by setting legal conditions on its continued existence, the statement was a political declaration which did not set forth legal obligations. For example, the treaty would not automatically end if one or more of the objectives set forth in the statement were not achieved. In fact, few of the objectives set forth in the statement have been achieved as of July 2004, nine years later.

The Statement of Principles and Objectives pledged the NPT parties to work toward a number of objectives:

- reaffirmation of the Article 6 commitments of the nuclear weapon states to pursue eventual nuclear disarmament
- completion of the Comprehensive Test Ban Treaty (CTBT) by the end of 1996
- commencement of negotiations for a treaty to stop the manufacture of nuclear bomb material
- efforts by the nuclear weapon states to sharply reduce global nuclear arsenals
- encouragement of the creation of new nuclear-weapon-free zones
- vigorous pursuit of universality of membership in the NPT (most importantly, Israel, as well as India and Pakistan, who maintain nuclear weapon programs outside of the NPT)
- an enhanced IAEA verification system (which led to the IAEA Additional Protocol, discussed below)
- further steps beyond the security assurances that had already been given to assure the nonnuclear weapon states against the use or threat of use of nuclear weapons against them by the nuclear weapon states

There were several associated commitments: a commitment that progress toward the goals of the Statement of Principles and Objectives could be assessed more or less annually as part of the agreed treaty review process; national declarations of security assurances from the nuclear weapon states to the nonnuclear weapon states, and a resolution urging universal NPT membership in the Middle East (intended by the Arab states to be aimed at Israel). These various additional commitments, being seemingly responsive to some degree to the concerns of many NPT nonnuclear weapon states that permanent extension might weaken the NPT nuclear weapon states' commitment to disarmament, assured an over-

whelming majority for permanent or indefinite extension. However, there were still some twenty states that were unhappy even
with this settlement, for various reasons, such as the failure to make
the aforesaid security assurances legally binding, or the failure to
explicitly insist that Israel eventually join the treaty as a nonnuclear weapon state. Permanent extension was achieved, meaning
that the resolution legally making the treaty permanent was passed
on a no-objection basis. However, after passage of permanent
extension, a number of states made speeches criticizing this settlement (answered by an equal number of states expressing support for it). So a fragile consensus was achieved, and the NPT
became permanent.

When the international community met in 2000 to review the
progress of the member states in implementing the Statement of
Principles and Objectives, many nonnuclear weapon states
remained uncomfortable with the nuclear weapon states' commitment to their NPT obligations and to the obligations accepted
in 1995. The five-year period after the indefinite extension of
the NPT and before the NPT review conference planned for 2000
had witnessed numerous setbacks to the NPT regime, including
nuclear tests in South Asia by India and Pakistan, and Russia's
reemphasis of the possible first use of nuclear weapons in connection with its revised nuclear doctrine. No progress had been
made in nuclear weapon reductions between the United States
and Russia, and there had been only limited progress on the other
subjects addressed in the Statement of Principles and Objectives.

There was much criticism directed at the United States. Further, the U.S. Senate had rejected the CTBT, which France,
Britain, and Russia had all signed and ratified. France had scaled
back its submarine-launched ballistic missile force, completely
eliminated its ground-based nuclear arsenal, and dismantled its
nuclear test site. Britain had reduced its arsenal of deployed strategic nuclear weapons to a level lower than that of any other NPT

nuclear weapon state, and had reduced the alert status of its remaining nuclear arsenal. Russia was pressing for reductions in U.S. and Russian strategic nuclear arsenals to 1,500 weapons or less—some in Moscow even urging the commencement of five-power discussions on reductions in strategic nuclear forces involving all five of the recognized nuclear weapon states. China maintained a minimalist nuclear deterrent. A number of additional states had joined the NPT, so that by 2000, of all the states in the world, only India, Pakistan, Israel, and Cuba remained nonparties. (Cuba joined in 2002, but North Korea withdrew in 2003.)

Nevertheless, against this backdrop, at the review conference in 2000, the parties agreed to a final document that set forth the agreed views of all the NPT member states on various NPT-related issues. This document reaffirmed the basic bargain of the NPT. Among its most important new commitments was the agreement on an "unequivocal undertaking" by the nuclear weapon states to accomplish the total elimination of nuclear weapons. This commitment lacked the references to "ultimate" or "general and complete" disarmament that had previously served to limit or condition the nuclear weapon states' pursuit of nuclear weapon elimination. While its precise interpretation differed among the NPT parties, it is clear that the final document made maintenance of the Anti-Ballistic Missile Treaty an NPT-related undertaking. While the final document did not contain legal obligations, it did set forth important agreed-upon declarations of the member states, considered to be politically binding in good faith. (The U.S. withdrawal from the ABM Treaty in 2002 was contrary to this undertaking.) In the document, the NPT parties also agreed to maintain the nuclear test moratorium, pending entry into force of the CTBT.

So, in 2000 the parties pulled a rabbit out of the hat. The NPT regime was held together by paste and a promise. But how much longer can this last? The barrier that has held for so long may be beginning to weaken. Each time it gets more and more difficult to demonstrate the commitment by the nuclear weapon states (particularly the United States) to uphold their end of the deal. North Korea has withdrawn from the NPT and claims to be building nuclear weapons. Recent intelligence estimates published in newspapers suggest that North Korea may now possess up to eight nuclear weapons. North Korea apparently received uranium enrichment technology from the A. Q. Khan network, and the United States has asserted that North Korea is also seeking nuclear weapons through the uranium enrichment route. Iran is suspected of having a nuclear weapon program and Iran admitted in late 2003 to being in violation of its IAEA safeguards agreement by failing to report its acquisition of uranium enrichment technology (possibly from the Khan network). While denying an intent to acquire nuclear weapons, Iran promised future cooperation with the IAEA and said it would "temporarily" suspend uranium enrichment activities. In February of 2004, trace quantities of HEU were discovered by the IAEA at an Iranian site. In June 2004, Iran ended this temporary suspension.

On the other hand, Libya, another recipient of uranium enrichment from the Khan network, has renounced its rudimentary nuclear weapon program (as well as its much more advanced chemical weapons program), turned over to the United States the equipment it purchased from Khan, and pledged full support of the NPT and the IAEA. It has now been conclusively demonstrated that Iraq did not resuscitate its nuclear program, which was destroyed by the IAEA after the first Gulf War.

The NPT regime has not yet failed. However, as U.S. nonproliferation policy continues to seemingly drift toward policies that could break the NPT—for example, resumption of nuclear testing and declaring a policy of possibly using nuclear weapons against NPT nonnuclear weapon states—the cost of holding the regime together gets higher and higher. Despite the United States' traditional leadership in nonproliferation efforts and its specific and tangible interest in the success of those efforts, it is no longer clear that nonproliferation is U.S. policy. The Senate rejection of the CTBT, the decision to withdraw from the ABM Treaty and to promptly deploy a national missile defense which could include space-based elements, and implications of a return to nuclear testing suggest either that nonproliferation is not U.S. policy, or that the United States is being cavalier about its security interests.

To those that support a strictly unilateralist course of action for the United States, the cost of maintaining the nonproliferation regime may be too high. Our membership in a variety of international instruments associated with the NPT regime, negotiations of additional treaties and the constraints associated with them, efforts to move toward significant reductions in nuclear arsenals, and suggestions from NATO allies that NATO should move to a core deterrence policy and forswear the first use of nuclear weapons are seen by some as a high price to pay for nonproliferation.

If we do not want to pay that price, if we do not take the steps required to strengthen the NPT regime, then we can expect to continue to drift toward a widely proliferated world. This would be a most unfortunate development for U.S. security. But if this is the path on which we will ultimately travel, then we must be prepared to cope with the new security challenges associated with it. We would need to reevaluate our fundamental strategic interests and reconsider our criteria for interventions abroad. Perhaps we would need to broaden our list of potential targets for nuclear weapons; field a larger, more diverse nuclear arsenal; and return to testing new types of nuclear weapons.

But if a world in which every conflict has the potential to "go nuclear" is not what we want, then the United States must take steps to avoid it. We must strengthen the NPT. That means first and foremost taking the necessary steps to ratify the CTBT and then working towards its full implementation.

The United States must make serious efforts at the Conference on Disarmament in Geneva to jump-start negotiations for a treaty stopping the production of nuclear bomb material. Just as the CTBT was the only objective given a specific timeline for completion in the 1995 Statement of Principles and Objectives, demonstrating its importance to the international community, the 2000 final document set 2005 as a target date for completion of such a treaty banning the production of fissile material. Meeting this goal at this juncture is probably impossible, but the United States should make every responsible effort to achieve it.

The United States should be mindful of its obligations under NPT Article 4 to promote the peaceful uses of nuclear energy and to assist nonnuclear weapon states in their utilization of these technologies consistent with nonproliferation commitments. One way to do this would be to promote the development of proliferation-resistant nuclear energy technologies.

The United States should continue to work with the Russian government to expand and improve programs intended to secure nuclear materials and expertise in the former Soviet Union. The danger of nuclear weapons, fissile material, or scientific expertise becoming available to unstable regimes or terrorist organizations is too great to act otherwise.

The United States and Russia should pursue truly deep cuts in strategic nuclear arsenals, not just a reduction in those operationally deployed. In recent years, the Russians have proposed nuclear weapon reductions in the context of a new strategic arms reduction agreement to as few as 1,500 strategic nuclear warheads. The United States rejected this suggestion in 2001 and instead proposed the course reflected in the 2002 Treaty of Moscow, which required no actual reductions in strategic nuclear weapons. If the NPT regime is to be preserved for the long term, it will be important for the United States and Russia to reduce their arsenals to the lowest levels possible consistent with security and stability, and for the other nuclear weapon states to become part of this process.

The United States, NATO, Russia, and the rest of the nuclear weapon states should adopt core deterrence postures whereby the sole role of nuclear weapons would be to deter the use of other nuclear weapons. By adopting policies pursuant to which they would under no circumstances be the first to introduce nuclear weapons into a conflict, the nuclear weapon states would eliminate potential inconsistencies between their policies on the potential use of nuclear weapons and the negative security assurances made in conjunction with the extension of the NPT (the following chapter discusses this issue in more detail).

The United States should seek to achieve widespread adherence to the IAEA enhanced nuclear safeguards embodied in the IAEA Additional Protocol (an amendment to the NPT safeguards agreements), developed in 1997 in response to concerns about verifying nonnuclear weapon states' compliance with their NPT obligations that arose as a result of events in Iraq and North Korea. The enhanced safeguards in the protocol would enable the IAEA to use environmental monitoring techniques to detect trace amounts of residue left behind during the enrichment of uranium and the manufacture of plutonium. For these safeguards to be implemented, however, each individual NPT party is required to sign and subsequently ratify the Additional Protocol. To date, approximately eighty nations have signed the protocol, but only about thirty-five such agreements have entered into force. The United States has recently ratified the protocol and has taken the lead in encouraging worldwide adherence. Iran signed in December 2003.

And, finally, the fundamental question of NPT universality remains to be addressed, much less resolved. The perceived credibility and effectiveness of the NPT is a measure of the strength of the entire nonproliferation regime, and rests on the treaty being applied universally. Nonnuclear weapon states have questioned the wisdom of adhering to the NPT when India, Pakistan, and Israel all operate outside the treaty and leave the regime incomplete. With Cuba's accession to the NPT in 2002, only these three states remain outside the NPT regime (except for North Korea, which, having withdrawn from the NPT in 2003, is essentially a NPT compliance case). While there is no likelihood that India, Pakistan, or Israel will give up their nuclear weapon programs or that the NPT will be amended to admit them as nuclear weapon states in the foreseeable future, some way needs to be found to link these three states to the NPT regime so that a dialogue can at least begin.

On February 11, 2004, President George W. Bush outlined a seven-point U.S. program aimed at discouraging nuclear proliferation. Perhaps the most significant proposal was that the forty-nation Nuclear Suppliers Group (a voluntary regime which includes the world's leading exporters of nuclear technologies, equipment, and materials) refuse to sell uranium-enrichment and nuclear waste reprocessing equipment to NPT nonnuclear weapon states without such technology that do not promise never to acquire it, and that in compensation, nuclear exporters ensure that nations have "reliable access at reasonable cost to fuel for civilian reactors." The president asserted that the NPT guaranteed access to nuclear technology to NPT nonnuclear states and that this was a "loophole" which had been exploited by North Korea and Iran to pursue weapon programs. While this is unquestionably a problem, the president's proposal is a de facto revision of the NPT basic bargain, which restricts NPT nonnuclear states' access to nuclear technology while showing no movement toward nuclear disarmament on the part of the nuclear weapon states. Since this prospect will not only disadvantage Iran, but also states such as Brazil, and since it suggests no progress on disarmament, it probably will not be effective. The president also proposed making the signing of the IAEA Additional Protocol for enhanced inspection by next year a condition for nuclear trade. However, at the time, only about 20 percent of NPT parties had joined the protocol, which was negotiated in 1997. The president recommended an expansion of the Proliferation Security Initiative, designed to make it more feasible to, among other things, stop ships on the high seas and search them for weapons of mass destruction (WMD). This program looks increasingly promising.

The day after the president's speech, in a statement to the press, the Director-General of the IAEA, Mohamed ElBaradei, while recognizing the problem, proposed instead that a new protocol to the NPT be developed in order to bring the nuclear fuel cycle (including uranium enrichment and nuclear waste reprocessing) under multinational control, with appropriate checks and balances. ElBaradei emphasized that a fundamental part of the basic bargain is the commitment of the five NPT nuclear weapon states to move toward disarmament, saying that "we must abandon the unworkable notion that it is morally reprehensible for some countries to pursue weapons of mass destruction and acceptable for others to rely on them for security. . . . If the world does not change course, we risk self-destruction."

5

The Political Value
of Nuclear Weapons

IN THE EARLY YEARS OF THE COLD WAR, NATO was composed of countries seriously weakened—in some cases, virtually destroyed—as a result of World War II, who were confronted across the inner German divide (the line between NATO-governed West Germany and Soviet-controlled East Germany) by massively superior Soviet and Warsaw Pact conventional forces. It was feared that these forces could overrun Western Europe in a matter of days, and NATO governments did not have the financial strength to put sizable forces in the field. U.S. forces were present in Europe in significant numbers throughout the Cold War, but even with the U.S. forces, NATO forces were significantly inferior to the Warsaw Pact forces arrayed on the other side; the disparity in battle tanks, for example, was three to one.

To redress this imbalance, the United States and NATO adopted a policy of holding open the possibility of employing tactical nuclear weapons to halt a massive Warsaw Pact assault. The United

States deployed up to 7,000 tactical or short-range nuclear weapons in Europe, which undoubtedly helped to keep the peace and alleviate Soviet pressure on Western Europe. While NATO likely would only have resorted to nuclear weapons in extremis, the Soviets could never be sure. Because of the threat of escalation to strategic nuclear war and of putting itself at risk, it was uncertain whether the United States would ever actually use these weapons. The question was often raised, "Would the United States risk New York to save Paris?" President Charles de Gaulle didn't think so. He withdrew France from the NATO Nuclear Planning Group and initiated the French nuclear weapon program. Thus, during the Cold War, the massive conventional superiority of the Warsaw Pact in Central Europe was offset in part by U.S. and NATO nuclear weapons. However, in the post–Cold War world, it is NATO that now has the conventional force preponderance in Europe — by a two-to-one margin over the East.

Due to the ongoing confrontation during the Cold War, there were limits to what could be accomplished to redeem the NPT arms control commitment of the nuclear weapon states. The political value of nuclear weapons was very high. To be considered a great power in the post–World War II world, a state needed to possess nuclear weapons; to be considered a superpower (as were the United States and the Soviet Union) required the possession of thousands of nuclear weapons. Now, years after the end of the Cold War, the value of nuclear weapons remains very high. Although it is an historical accident, the five NPT nuclear weapon states are the five permanent members of the Security Council of the United Nations. Often referred to as the P-5, these states — the United States, Britain, France, Russia, and China — are considered in many respects to be the world's most influential states. This preeminence in influence seems to some degree keyed to the possession of nuclear weapons authorized by the NPT. A former Indian foreign minister has referred to this situation as "nuclear apartheid." The purpose of NPT Article 6 and the 1995 Statement of Principles and Objectives was to redress this perceived discrimination within the NPT regime. If the nonproliferation objectives thus set forth are to succeed, there must be a reduction in the political value of nuclear weapons. Otherwise, these weapons will, over the long run, be too attractive (and the fifty-year-old technology involved too simple) to control, and the NPT will ultimately fail.

The SALT negotiations during the 1970s between the United States and the Soviet Union put the first limitations on the nuclear arms race, in effect placing an upper limit on strategic nuclear missiles and bombers (the delivery vehicles of strategic nuclear warheads) and agreeing on the first reductions. The START negotiations in the 1980s and 1990s between the United States and Russia produced the START I and START II Treaties, which established significant reductions in nuclear missiles and bombers. The START I Treaty, which was signed in 1991 and entered into force in 1994, reduced these weapons to a level of approximately 50 percent of the Cold War high. The START II Treaty signed by President George H. W. Bush in 1993 would have carried these reductions to two-thirds of the Cold War maximum, but it never became effective. Presidents Bill Clinton and Boris Yeltsin signed a framework agreement in 1997, which, if it had been implemented, would have carried this process still further (an approximate 40 percent reduction from START II levels), but due to political difficulties in the administration in the late 1990s related to the struggle over missile defense, it was never translated into a treaty. With the 2002 Treaty of Moscow, which called for significant operational reductions of weapons in the field (but not before 2012), the strategic arms control process seems to have been abandoned. The START II Treaty has been put aside and, according to U.S. government statements, the minimal limitations contained in the Treaty of Moscow will not be followed by additional measures.

For the United States and Russia to carry out their NPT Article 6 disarmament obligations, the strategic arms reduction process or something like it must be revived, with serious attempts to reach significant and effective additional reductions in nuclear weapons. There has been more progress in arms control since the end of the Cold War than during it, but much more must be accomplished if the NPT regime is to remain viable.

A striking example of the kind of thinking that could ultimately threaten the NPT regime was given by British Prime Minister Harold Macmillan in a television interview in February 1958 in reference to the British nuclear weapon program. He spoke of how "the independent contribution [i.e., British nuclear weapons] . . . puts us where we ought to be, in the position of a great power." In a speech in November 1961, French president Charles de Gaulle said that "a great state" that does not have nuclear weapons when others do "does not command its own destiny." After the May 1998 Indian nuclear tests, Indian Prime Minister Atal Behari Vajpayee announced, "We have a big bomb now, India is a nuclear weapon state" (*Manchester Guardian*, May 24, 1998, p. 3). Even the Dalai Lama, who is opposed to nuclear weapons, is quoted in the same article as saying, "Some big countries say only they have the right to nuclear weapons. India is a big country and in that case it should have the right." Clearly, the belief held by nonnuclear weapon states that some nuclear weapon states cling to nuclear weapons as their claim to great power status is not without foundation.

The long-term security of the United States will depend on de-emphasizing the political significance of nuclear weapons. In the 1997 report referred to earlier, entitled *The Future of U.S. Nuclear Weapons Policy*, the U.S. National Academy of Sciences, a nongovernmental, highly prominent professional organization of U.S. scientists, suggested some important practical steps that the United States should take to de-emphasize the role of nuclear weapons and to minimize the risk they constitute. The report recommends that U.S. and Russian nuclear forces be reduced to much lower levels and limited to the "core deterrence" role of simply discouraging the use of nuclear weapons by other states. The academy further recommends that as part of limiting nuclear weapons to their "core deterrence" function, the United States adopt a "no-first-use" policy of not initiating the use of nuclear weapons or introducing nuclear weapons in any future conflict, and limiting by doctrine any use of nuclear weapons to retaliation for nuclear weapon use by others. No-first-use is a particularly significant issue to focus on because it could be implemented immediately. An explicit, clearly enunciated policy of not introducing nuclear weapons into future conflicts would go a long way toward validating the good faith of the United States concerning its NPT nuclear arms control and disarmament commitments, and would reinforce the defensive posture of U.S. nuclear forces, making it clear that the sole purpose of the nuclear arsenal is to deter the use of nuclear weapons by others.

A no-first-use agreement would be an important step toward demonstrating to the nonnuclear weapon states that the nuclear weapon states take their disarmament commitments seriously. It would mean that in a crisis, no nuclear weapon state would consider a policy of striking another nuclear weapon state with a nuclear weapon and that the five NPT nuclear weapon states would honor their NPT commitments to in effect never use nuclear weapons against NPT nonnuclear weapon states.

A no-first-use policy was not made part of the *Nuclear Posture Review* (a report published every few years by the Department of Defense on nuclear weapon plans and doctrines) in 1994. Neither was it made part of the December 2001 *Nuclear Posture Review* (NPR), which instead raised the political value of nuclear weapons by suggesting their possible use not only against Russia and China, but also against North Korea, Iran, Iraq, Syria, and Libya—at the time, all nonnuclear weapon state parties to the NPT. The 2001 NPR also implied the continued possession of nuclear weapons for many decades by discussing the projected advent of new nuclear weapon delivery systems some twenty-five to thirty years into the future. It has been suggested publicly by former U.S. government officials that the rationale for not adopting a no-first-use policy was the argument that if the United States adopted a no-first-use policy, then close U.S. allies, especially those considered to be under the U.S. "nuclear umbrella" (protected by the deterrence capability of U.S. nuclear weapons), such as Germany and Japan, would lose confidence in the nuclear deterrence extended to them by the United States and would proceed to build their own nuclear weapons. Government officials in Germany and Japan, however, have indicated informally that neither the adoption of a no-first-use policy nor the negotiation of deep cuts in a balanced context with the other nuclear weapon states would undermine their confidence in the commitment of the United States to their defense. On the contrary, efforts to reduce the political significance attached to nuclear weapons, such as the adoption of a no-first-use policy, would serve as an added reinforcement to the nuclear nonproliferation commitments of these countries. A no-first-use agreement among the five nuclear weapon states would be an even more important step because it would reinforce NPT-related national political statements and end any dispute over whether or not the first use of nuclear weapons violates international law.

Failure to adopt a no-first-use policy should not be justified by suggestions that nuclear weapons should be used to explicitly deter chemical or biological weapon attacks. Not only would such a strategy be inappropriate and disproportionate, it would also endanger the NPT regime. The way to deal with threats of the use of chemical and biological weapons is with the overwhelming conventional power of the United States and of NATO. It should be made clear that any state that resorts to chemical or biological weapons will pay an unbearable price. To threaten retaliation with nuclear weapons would only encourage countries to seek their own nuclear weapon capability, and, of course, the widespread proliferation of nuclear weapons would neutralize the existing conventional superiority of the United States and NATO.

Some have argued that it was the veiled threat to use nuclear weapons in retaliation that deterred Iraq from using chemical and biological weapons in the first Gulf War in 1991. But memoirs since published by President George Bush, National Security Advisor Brent Scowcroft, Secretary of State James A. Baker, and General Colin Powell reveal that the United States had appropriately ruled out use of such weapons under any circumstances in war against Iraq. To make such a threat in the future would risk the calling of a bluff, and put pressure on an American president to authorize the use of nuclear weapons—the last thing we should want. The pledge made by the United States, Britain, and the Soviet Union at the first United Nations special session on disarmament in 1978 not to use nuclear weapons against a non-nuclear weapon state party to the NPT (unless it conducts an attack in alliance with a nuclear weapon state) makes no exception for chemical or biological weapons. Numerous nonnuclear weapon states made their decision to join the NPT after this commitment was announced.

These pledges, or "negative security assurances," were reaffirmed in April 1995 by the five nuclear weapon states in the context of the 1995 NPT Review and Extension Conference, and were an essential part of the agreement to indefinitely extend the NPT. Achieving legally binding negative security assurances from the five NPT nuclear weapon states was a major objective for many NPT nonnuclear weapon states at the 1995 conference, and was reiterated several times in position papers of the "nonaligned" or third world states. Even though the negative security assurances actually given in April 1995 by the NPT nuclear weapon states fell short of this objective in that they were national policy statements and not legally binding commitments, the texts were adopted pursuant to a unanimously approved formal UN security council resolution. Without those commitments, the indefinite extension of the NPT may not have taken place. Without question, the then 173 (now 182) nonnuclear weapon state parties to the NPT agreed to its indefinite extension relying on these commitments.

At the Review and Extension Conference, United States Secretary of State Warren Christopher delivered the U.S. pledge that it would not use nuclear weapons against any NPT nonnuclear weapon state party to the NPT "except in the case of an invasion or an attack on the United States, its territories, its armed forces or other troops, its allies, or on a State toward which it has a security commitment, carried out or sustained by such a nonnuclear weapon State in association or alliance with a nuclear weapon State." To sum up U.S. policy, the United States retained the right to use nuclear weapons first only if engaged in a military conflict with another nuclear weapon state, a state not party to the NPT, or an NPT nonnuclear weapon state attacking the United States in alliance with a nuclear weapon state. France, Britain, and Russia offered similar negative security assurances, which were subsequently harmonized and submitted as the underlying basis of UN Security Council resolution 984 on security assurances supporting NPT extension. Since China has consistently maintained an unequivocal no-first-use policy toward all states as a part of its nuclear doctrine since its first nuclear test—the ultimate negative security assurance—it did not need to issue a separate statement in 1995.

As said, the negative security assurances offered in the context of the 1995 Review and Extension Conference were a critical part of the quid pro quo for the indefinite extension of the NPT, and remain crucial to the viability of the regime. After all, if a nonnuclear weapon state is going to permanently forswear nuclear weapons, the least it can expect from its nuclear weapon state treaty partners is that it will not be attacked by them using nuclear weapons. Further, the five nuclear weapon states have signed legally binding protocols to the nuclear-weapon-free zone treaties for Latin America, the South Pacific, and Africa, comprising some ninety nations. In these protocols, the nuclear weapon states have undertaken never to use or threaten to use nuclear weapons against nuclear-weapon-free zone treaty parties. The World Court, in its 1996 advisory opinion referred to above, found the NPT-related negative security assurances, given their importance to NPT extension, to be commitments that should be considered just as binding as those undertaken in connection with nuclear-weapon-free zone treaties, even though they are national political statements and not treaty commitments, and that the threat of use and the use of nuclear weapons must be subject to international law. The World Court also ruled in 1996 that any use of nuclear weapons would generally contravene the principles and rules of international humanitarian law (e.g., the rule of proportionality and the requirement that weapons not be indiscriminate as to civilian casualties)—except, possibly, in a circumstance of extreme self-defense where the survival of the nation was in question (the court was split on this, 7-7). Such a circumstance could not occur for a nuclear weapon state in the absence of a threat of use or the actual use of nuclear weapons.

While the NATO nuclear weapon states (United States, Britain, France) have all extended negative security assurances to nonnuclear weapon states, the NATO alliance, continuing the policy it used to contain the Soviet Union in Europe, maintains that it could use nuclear weapons first in the event of an attack against any state. Thus, on the one hand, the United States, Britain, and France, as NPT nuclear weapon states, in effect have pledged never to use nuclear weapons against NPT nonnuclear weapon states;

on the other hand, as members of NATO, these three states retain the right to introduce nuclear weapons into future conflicts, presumably against both nonnuclear and nuclear weapon states. The United States, Britain, and France have national policies to the same effect, as exemplified for the United States by the December 2001 *Nuclear Posture Review*. The United States cloaks this policy with respect to nonnuclear weapon states in a doctrine of "calculated ambiguity," in which it simply reserves all options — a policy that is not consistent with the NPT negative security assurances commitment. Russia recently has formally adopted the same national policy.

This inconsistency is not simply a matter of international law. It serves to promote nuclear proliferation in that it devalues the NPT and accordingly undermines NATO security. To suggest that the NATO Alliance, the most powerful conventional force in history (or the United States, the most militarily dominant country that the world has ever seen, based solely on its conventional force capability), needs the threat of retaliation with nuclear weapons to deter, for example, the biological weapons of Syria, raises the question as to why Iran or Egypt or virtually anyone else does not need them as well. Retaining a first-use option for nuclear weapons for NATO, U.S., British, and French national policy as well as for Russian national policy suggests that these weapons are essential to the security and greatness of a state. Some see the possession of nuclear weapons as part of the definition of a state that has a permanent seat on the UN Security Council. But no rationale remains for the nuclear weapon states to retain the right to introduce nuclear weapons into a conflict. Clinging to the doctrine of the past supports the political value of nuclear weapons, undermines security, and undermines efforts to persuade nonnuclear weapon states to continue to refrain from developing nuclear weapons. Retaining the option to use nuclear weapons first reinforces the high political value already attributed to them, thereby making nonproliferation more difficult to achieve.

Religious leaders have denounced the doctrine of nuclear deterrence in today's world. Roman Catholic Archbishop Renato Martino of the Holy See said at the United Nations some years ago that "nuclear weapons are incompatible with the peace we seek for the twenty-first century." In June 1998, the Conference of the Catholic Bishops of the United States of America released a statement in which they said that "nuclear deterrence as a national policy must be condemned as morally abhorrent because it is the excuse and justification for the continued possession and further development of these horrendous weapons. We urge all to join in taking up the challenge to begin the effort to eliminate nuclear weapons now, rather than relying on them indefinitely."

In the short term, nothing would do more to lower the political value of nuclear weapons and thereby strengthen the NPT regime than a pledge by the United States, Britain, France, Russia, and the NATO Alliance that they will not introduce nuclear weapons into future conflicts. The present option to use nuclear weapons first does not serve any security purpose; on the contrary, if it does not change and the importance of nuclear weapons continues to be underscored by the United States, and to a lesser degree by Russia, it could contribute to increasing the threat of proliferation. If the United States continues to insist that it must explicitly retain the option to use nuclear weapons first, we are sending a clear message to the world: Nuclear weapons are essential to security and to being a first class state. The nations of the world are beginning to understand this message, and before long, it may be impossible to convince them otherwise.

6

Stopping Nuclear
Explosions: The Test Ban

F ROM THE EARLIEST OF TIMES, AFTER THE completion of the negotiation of the NPT in 1968, the NPT nonnuclear weapon states emphasized that the number one quid for their quo of renouncing nuclear weapons was an end to nuclear weapon tests—that is, a Comprehensive Nuclear-Test-Ban Treaty. This has been reiterated at every NPT review conference since, and was an express condition of the indefinite extension of the NPT in 1995.

At the NPT Review and Extension Conference in 1995, the United States and the other four NPT nuclear weapon parties agreed that they would complete negotiation of the CTBT by 1996. This was probably the single most important promise made to gain wide support from nonnuclear weapon states for making the NPT permanent. It was for many nations a test of the sincerity of the United States and the other NPT nuclear weapon states with respect to their NPT obligations. Many nonnuclear weapon parties have long relied upon the CTBT to reduce what they perceive as NPT-authorized discrimination against them.

This commitment was met, and the Comprehensive Nuclear-Test-Ban Treaty was signed in 1996. It established a complete and worldwide ban on all nuclear test explosions and provided for a vast international monitoring system composed of hundreds of seismic stations and other technical stations spread all over the world. President Bill Clinton was the first official to sign the treaty, at the ceremony at the United Nations; 171 other countries have since signed. One hundred and fourteen countries have ratified the treaty, including Britain, France, Russia, and Japan. However, it has not yet come into force. The treaty provides that all countries with nuclear facilities on their territories must ratify it for it to come into effect, and only thirty-one of the required forty-four have done so. The U.S. Senate rejected the CTBT in 1999, and there are no plans to call for its reconsideration by the Senate in the foreseeable future. The CTBT is overwhelmingly in the security interests of the United States. It would be verifiable, and would in no way diminish the reliability and effectiveness of the U.S. nuclear stockpile. The United States currently has a significant advantage over Russia and China—and indeed the rest of the world—in terms of the sophistication of its nuclear arsenal and the depth of knowledge possessed by its nuclear scientists. This advantage was developed by conducting well over 1,000 nuclear explosive tests (greater than the combined total of nuclear tests conducted by the rest of the world) and translates into a U.S. nuclear force of unmatched effectiveness. The Soviet Union and Russia conducted 715 tests; France, 210; and China, 45. Britain, which has had access to U.S. test data, has also conducted 45 tests.

A nuclear explosive testing program involving full-scale tests is necessary to provide confidence in the reliability of newly designed nuclear weapons, which are extremely complex. No responsible political leadership, no competent modern military authority, and no nation depending on nuclear weapons for its security could be expected to deploy a modern nuclear weapon without a full-scale test program. For its part, the United States has used on average six explosive tests before certifying its new weapon designs; France reportedly has used as many as twenty-two. Since under the Comprehensive Nuclear Test-Ban-Treaty no nation could conduct tests, it would not be possible for a state to develop a sophisticated nuclear arsenal. Thus, the CTBT would keep new designs for advanced weapons out of the stockpiles of Russia, China, and, of course, the United States, as well as other states with nuclear weapons. Under the CTBT, the U.S. arsenal would continue to consist of the world's most advanced weapons. No nation is better prepared to maintain the reliability of nuclear weapons, in a non-testing environment, than the United States. The information gathered by U.S. scientists through the nation's extensive nuclear testing program contributes to the effectiveness of the science-based Stockpile Stewardship Program which, if properly funded, will ensure that the safety and reliability of the U.S. nuclear arsenal will not erode over time. The leadership of the United States in the realm of supercomputer development, which is essential to the success of the SSP, further ensures this advantage. In effect, under the CTBT, no other nation would be as capable as the United States in maintaining its nuclear arsenal without testing.

When the U.S. Senate refused to give advice and consent to the CTBT in 1999, the most immediate effect on the NPT was to slow agreement by many NPT countries to the new, tougher IAEA inspections for all NPT nonnuclear weapon states. The director-general of the IAEA, Mohamed ElBaradei, later said in a press comment: "The Senate vote against the ban on nuclear tests was a devastating blow to our efforts to gain acceptance of more intrusive inspections of nuclear facilities around the world" (*Washington Post*, June 15, 2000). Following the Senate's vote on the CTBT, the ratification process of the Additional Protocol proceeded very slowly, and to date only about thirty-five NPT parties have actually brought it into force by ratifying it. In 2000, a senior IAEA expert explained that "innovations like this require diplomatic momentum, and without the United States in the lead, momentum disappears." He added that even "reliable countries are dragging their feet, asking why they should accept new burdens if America is turning its back on nuclear disarmament" (*Washington Post*, June 15, 2000). Until reliable countries accept the new IAEA safeguards, he said, the IAEA cannot put much pressure on suspect countries. The American ambassador to the IAEA commented that "the greatest danger is not that the NPT will dissolve but that it will atrophy" (*Washington Post*, June 15, 2000). Recently there has been a revival of interest in the Additional Protocol. Iran signed it in December 2003. And after consideration and approval by the Senate, the United States very recently ratified it. In his February 11, 2004, speech President Bush urged all nations that are "serious about proliferation" to approve the protocol.

Soon after that vote in 1999, according to Department of State officials who follow the foreign implementation of export controls required by the NPT, some NPT member states began acting as if the NPT requirements had been relaxed. These states appeared to be enforcing with less rigor NPT prohibitions on exports of nuclear materials, equipment, and related technologies to states that do not accept full-scope IAEA safeguards over their nuclear activities. These countries might have been saying, in effect, "If the United States is not going to enforce proliferation prevention measures such as the CTBT on itself, why should we enforce other nonproliferation requirements on ourselves?"

If the U.S. Senate is unwilling to approve the CTBT in the years ahead, and if the CTBT does not enter into force, to the detriment of both U.S. and international security, what could happen? The NPT, which has been critical both in constraining the spread of nuclear weapons to new nations and in rolling back proliferation in nuclear-weapon-capable countries such as Belarus, Kazakhstan, South Africa, Argentina, Brazil, and Ukraine, would be substantially weakened. If the United States does not ratify, then the CTBT will not go into effect for any country, because the United States is one of forty-four countries with nuclear facilities who must join in order for the treaty to go into effect. If the CTBT does not go into effect, India and Pakistan may well eventually resume nuclear testing. If India tests, China may use that and the failure of the United States to ratify as reasons for it to resume testing. China may want to produce smaller nuclear warheads so that its missiles can carry multiple warheads and decoys to confuse and overwhelm interceptor missiles from the U.S. national missile defense system. If China tests, and North Korea proceeds with an overt nuclear weapon program (as its recent behavior suggests), what would Japan and South Korea do?

Japan has been a leader in trying to bring the CTBT into force at the earliest possible date. But if India, Pakistan, and China resume testing; if North Korea has acquired nuclear weapons; and if the CTBT cannot go into effect because of the U.S. Senate rejection, how long might it be before some future Japanese government would consider a secret program to build nuclear weapons to protect itself? Japan felt threatened in 1998 by the combination of the Indian-Pakistan nuclear tests in May and the North Korean Taepodong I rocket that flew over Japan a few months later. A parliamentary vice-minister for defense in Japan was forced to resign in 1999 when he suggested that Japan build nuclear weapons after these events. Although officially Japan remains steadfastly against becoming a nuclear weapon state, the vice-minister was certainly not the only one in Japan with an opposing view. According to a provision of the NPT, Japan has the right to withdraw on three months' notice (as do other NPT states parties) "if it decides that extraordinary events, related to the subject matter of this treaty, have jeopardized the supreme interests of its country." Japan may believe it must respond to overt North Korean acquisition of nuclear weapons in any case, but if China, India, and Pakistan are all conducting nuclear weapon tests as well, the pressure on Japan would be recognizably greater.

If Japan withdrew from the NPT, would South Korea be far behind? South Korea has been invaded by both China and Japan in the past. It could well feel threatened by events in North Korea if China resumed testing and if Japan withdrew from the NPT. South Korea had a nuclear weapon program in the 1970s, but was dissuaded from pursuing it by the United States. If South Korea withdrew from the NPT, it could produce nuclear weapons in a short time. Taiwan also had an incipient nuclear-weapon-capable program in the 1970s. Thus a dangerous nuclear weapon spiral could be created in Northeast Asia.

Might results comparable to these take place in other parts of the world—the Middle East, for example? Of the states in the Middle East essential for entry into force, Egypt and Iran are likely to wait on Israel before ratifying, and Israel is likely to wait on the United States. Meanwhile, Iran is acquiring a nuclear power reactor from Russia and is constructing uranium enrichment facilities that were "temporarily" suspended, and both Iran and Egypt have trained nuclear experts. In June 2004, Iran formally announced that it was resuming construction of these facilities. These examples illustrate how the failure to bring the CTBT into force could contribute to the potential spread of nuclear weapons to several countries in the Middle East, and South and Northeast Asia, and perhaps elsewhere.

After the first Gulf War, as a result of Iraq's success in hiding its secret nuclear weapon activities, the United States helped lead an effort by the IAEA to strengthen NPT safeguards to detect clandestine activities in the territories of nonnuclear weapon parties. Stronger safeguards were finally adopted as policy by the 1997 IAEA Board of Governors and the General Conference in the form of an additional agreement amending the NPT safeguards agreement, referred to as the Additional Protocol (discussed above and in Chapter 4). Each NPT party had to sign and then ratify the amendment to its own IAEA safeguards agreement to make the tougher safeguards applicable to itself. Exceeding expectations at the time, some sixty countries signed the agreement, but the process slowed after the Senate vote on the CTBT.

U.S. failure to ratify the CTBT, in addition to substantially weakening the NPT and slowing the acceptance of stronger IAEA safeguards, would cast doubt on the credibility of the commitment in Article 6 of the NPT, to "negotiate in good faith on effective measures relating to the cessation of the nuclear arms race at an early date and to nuclear disarmament." In this context, "cessation of the nuclear arms race" meant, from the very beginning, the CTBT. This is made clear by the preamble of the NPT and from statements made by negotiating parties in 1968.

The end of the Cold War has signaled a dramatic change in the U.S. nuclear weapon program. The continuous cycle of developing, testing, and deploying new nuclear weapons has ended. During the Cold War, the United States conducted more nuclear weapon tests than the rest of the world combined. Recently, there have been arguments made in Washington that the United States should develop a new type of nuclear weapon that could burrow deep into the ground to destroy underground storage facilities. The concern is that rogue states might build storage facilities for chemical or biological weapons deep underground. This likely would be used to justify renewed nuclear test-

ing, despite a moratorium of seven-years duration on nuclear testing by the recognized nuclear weapon states. The U.S. nuclear
test site near Las Vegas is now a wasteland strewn with mangled
buildings and pockmarked with huge craters, evidence to the
more than 900 nuclear tests the government conducted there
between 1951 and 1992.

But there are other ways to destroy underground facilities, such
as high-yield conventional weapons (the United States currently
has a 15,000-pound bomb in its inventory) combined with a special forces attack. The problem with nuclear weapons is that it
appears likely that they will not be able to burrow deep enough
before exploding to contain the radioactive fallout that would be
caused by the nuclear explosion. Even the best-designed weapon
could only burrow thirty to fifty feet before exploding; to destroy
an underground facility buried 1,000 feet in rock would require
a 100-kiloton nuclear weapon. As demonstrated by the radioactive material vented into the atmosphere at the Nevada test site
in the past, thirty to fifty feet is not deep enough to contain the
radioactive fallout of such a weapon under the ground, and a 100-
kiloton nuclear explosion not so contained would throw an enormous amount of radioactively charged dirt into the atmosphere.
An attack with such a weapon on an underground storage facility for chemical weapons in Libya (an example often mentioned
in the past, but no longer relevant) could contaminate sizable parts
of Western Europe, given the winds that blow from the Sahara
Desert over Europe.

The United States now relies on an expanded program of stockpile stewardship for its nuclear arsenal, which is in the range of
10,000 weapons, to ensure that (1) the enduring arsenal remains
reliable, effective, and safe into the indefinite future without
nuclear explosive testing; (2) the United States maintains com-
petence in nuclear weapon technology; and (3) the United States

retains the technical capability and manufacturing infrastructure in order to respond, as required for U.S. security, to changed strategic circumstances.

Today, the nuclear weapons that are designed to remain in the enduring stockpile are — and will remain for the foreseeable future — effective, safe, and reliable. Confidence in today's stockpile is based on understanding gained from almost fifty years of stockpile surveillance, and the experience and analyses of a very large number of nuclear tests, including more than 150 nuclear tests of modern weapon types, over the past twenty-five to thirty years. The overwhelming majority of U.S. nuclear tests during the Cold War were devoted to developing new and more advanced warheads and weapons systems for deployment. Only a very small percentage (well under 10 percent of the underground nuclear explosive tests of modern weapons from 1972 to the end of U.S. testing in 1992) were stockpile confidence tests (i.e., tests conducted on currently deployed weapons to confirm confidence in them). That is fewer than one test per year for an arsenal of many thousands of weapons. President George H. W. Bush announced in 1992 that the United States does not need to develop new nuclear warhead designs for deployment. This decision opened up the possibility of the CTBT.

Under international law (the Vienna Convention on the Law of Treaties), every signatory to the CTBT is legally bound not to conduct nuclear explosive tests, pending ratification, unless it formally announces that it will not ratify. The current testing moratorium by the five recognized nuclear weapon states (which, for the United States, has been in effect since 1992) is, at present, only a political commitment. When the CTBT comes into force, this political commitment will become legally binding, thereby legitimizing a range of actions by the international community in support of the ban and, if necessary, in response to a possible nuclear test by any nuclear-weapon-capable nation.

With regard to verification concerns, the CTBT will ensure that all parties will have considerably more information about what is happening at U.S., Russian, and Chinese tests sites. The International Monitoring System (IMS) established pursuant to the CTBT will enhance efforts to monitor international nuclear explosive test activities. The new system will consist of 321 monitoring stations around the world, some 47 percent of which are now complete (a significant number in Russia and China), augmenting the existing capabilities that exist in the United States and elsewhere. The CTBT will also formally establish a regime for on-site inspection, and will be the first truly high-tech arms control treaty verification regime relying on seismic monitoring, radionuclide sensing (monitoring airborne radioactive particles), a hydroacoustic network (to monitor possible underwater explosions), and an infrasound network (to monitor sound waves) thereby to effectively monitor underground, underwater, and in the atmosphere on a worldwide basis.

There remains, nevertheless, concern among U.S. opponents of the test ban that nations would be able to hide nuclear explosive tests in environments that would mask their seismic signatures or otherwise prevent their detection. Only nations with advanced nuclear testing programs and extensive underground testing experience are likely to be able to conduct such deceptive tests, whose preparation and yields would have to be carefully controlled. This would rule out India, Pakistan, and Israel, as well as the so-called "states of proliferation concern" such as Iran and North Korea. Britain cannot conduct any tests as long as the U.S. test site is closed, as it has nowhere else to test. France has not tested on its European territory and has closed its test facilities in the South Pacific. As a result, U.S. concern about such deceptive measures can realistically only be directed toward Russia and China. Whatever the shortcomings of the IMS in this regard may be, the United States will be better able to monitor suspicious activities at Chinese, Russian, and other test sites with the CTBT and IMS in force than without.

This is not to say that detecting small deceptive nuclear tests of less than one kiloton will be easy. The assumption that, as an open society, the United States would not be able to perform tests deceptively could be translated into a strategic disadvantage for the United States. Russia and China might be able to evade detection while conducting a few low-yield tests (at one-half kiloton, for example), which could confer some marginal benefits, but these would be meaningful only if testing went undetected over a long period of time—which would not be possible to hide. Six IMS stations detected the Kara Sea seismic event near Novaya Zemlya in 1997, which had a 3.5 magnitude on the Richter scale, corresponding to a nuclear explosion with a yield of less than 1 kiloton. This is a good indication that the IMS, which has been significantly improved since that event and which will continue to be upgraded, can reasonably be expected to detect even very low-level events in regions of concern.

Article 14 of the CTBT makes some forty-four states necessary parties to the entry into force of the treaty. This number includes the five NPT-recognized nuclear weapon states, as well as India, Pakistan, Israel, and North Korea. Britain, France, Russia, and Japan (another important state in this process) have ratified the treaty. Several years ago, India promised that it would seriously consider CTBT ratification; this would have brought along Pakistan as well. Understandably, however, India made clear that it considered itself "off the hook" after the 1999 U.S. Senate vote rejecting the CTBT. China and Israel are waiting for U.S. ratification.

North Korea has of course taken no step to ratify the CTBT and has recently renounced the NPT. It has restarted its nuclear reactor and dismissed IAEA inspectors from the country. North Korea has the capability to reprocess the approximately 8,000 spent nuclear fuel rods that it now possesses in a relatively short time and acquire enough plutonium for five to six nuclear weapons. Current intelligence reported in the news media indicates that it has done so and may have built up to eight nuclear weapons, and the operation of its reactor will produce more spent fuel rods in the future. This is an alarming situation, but one which still may be capable of being resolved positively. What is needed are direct U.S.-North Korea negotiations in which Washington would consider giving North Korea what it seems to want: diplomatic recognition, a security guarantee, economic assistance, and trade opportunities. These would not be a great sacrifice. Time is on our side with respect to the eventual peaceful resolution of the long-standing confrontation on the Korean peninsula. In exchange, the United States should insist on, among other things, a verifiable end to all programs in North Korea related to nuclear weapons development, with IAEA inspectors on the ground; the return of North Korea to the NPT; and, eventually, North Korean CTBT ratification.

It is important for U.S. security that we ratify the CTBT, permitting its entry into force and saving a threatened NPT. This could be part of the return of the United States to its historic mission of pursuing a world community based on cooperation, mutual security, and international law and treaty arrangements.

7

Missile Defense

TODAY'S NATIONAL MISSILE DEFENSE POLICY is part of an increasing trend in the United States in the early years of the twenty-first century toward a unilateralist "go it alone" approach to national security. Our policy seems to reflect nostalgia for a bygone era in which the United States was insulated against threats to its national security by expansive oceans to the east and west and friendly neighbors to the north and south.

The merits and drawbacks of ballistic missile defense have been debated since the late 1960s, and domestic politics has dominated that debate. To some in Washington, D.C., national missile defense represents a resurrection of the dream of absolute security. Others see it as fueling the arms race, arguing that as defenses are built up they will be offset by more offensive forces on the other side, and so on (the concept of "arms race stability"). They also see it as destabilizing the nuclear arms race in that it encourages striking first in a crisis. For instance, if "country A" builds missile defenses against "country B," "country B" might come to believe that "country A" was planning to conduct a first strike and to utilize its defenses to ward off a weakened retaliatory strike; therefore, "country B" has to be sure to strike first in a crisis (the concept of "crisis stability"). The missile defense issue was settled for many years on the basis of ensuring arms control and crisis stability. However, over time the idea of seeking absolute security became stronger.

The North American Aerospace Defense Command (NORAD) was established in the 1950s with the mission of protecting the North American continent from bomber attack, and an early-warning radar line was deployed in northern Canada. But air defense seemed to become increasing irrelevant as it became clear that the weapon which actually threatened North America was the long-range ballistic missile carrying nuclear weapons. Thus, air defense was allowed to slowly decline, and when the ABM Treaty precluded any significant missile defense, NORAD became largely an early-warning organization.

The first U.S. ballistic missile interceptor systems were to be placed in cities, so as to defend them, and were to be armed with nuclear warheads. Once this became known, however, there were citizen revolts around the country. No one wanted nuclear weapons anywhere near them. The next idea was presented by then Secretary of Defense Robert McNamara in a 1967 speech in San Francisco. McNamara suggested that in place of a nationwide city defense or "thick system," involving the deployment of thousands of nuclear-tipped defensive missiles around the country to protect the United States from intercontinental ballistic missiles launched from the Soviet Union (which by then had many hundreds — soon to be thousands — of such missiles, all carrying large nuclear warheads), the United States would build a thin nationwide ballistic missile defense involving perhaps 100 or so defensive missiles to defend against Chinese long-range nuclear missiles (then nonexistent). This would entail the deployment of far fewer interceptor systems, and therefore far fewer irate citizens, but would still permit the deployment of a missile defense system—whether useful or not.

With city defense ruled out, and an anti-Chinese system seen as faintly ridiculous, the incoming Nixon administration proposed that instead of defending cities, the United States locate its missile defense systems at the air force bases where its strategic offensive intercontinental missiles were deployed. The argument was that defending these missiles assured us that the Soviet Union could not launch a massive preemptive nuclear strike, destroying our land-based long-range offensive missile forces and thereby rendering us vulnerable. Such an attack was always an unlikely scenario, and, in any case, the United States would still have had its strategic nuclear bombers and submarines with long-range nuclear missiles, which could devastate the Soviet Union in a retaliatory strike. This was called the Safeguard missile defense system, and it was to consist of both short- and long-range missile-interceptor missiles carrying large nuclear warheads. The interceptor missiles would only have to get near any incoming Soviet nuclear warheads to destroy them. Had this defensive system ever been used, it would, of course, have caused huge nuclear explosions in the upper atmosphere and in near space, and great damage on the ground.

In 1967, President Lyndon B. Johnson met with Soviet Premier Aleksey Kosygin in Glassboro, New Jersey, in the first U.S.-Soviet summit meeting in several years. President Johnson proposed a ban on strategic defensive systems (anti-ballistic missile systems designed to defend against long-range strategic nuclear missiles) so that the vast ongoing offensive nuclear arms race could be brought to an end. If there were no defensive systems, then neither side would need more strategic missiles, or so the idea went. Kosygin countered with a question: Why prohibit defense when it is strategic offensive systems that are the threat?

There the issue remained for several years, even after the beginning of the Strategic Arms Limitation Talks (SALT) between the
United States and the Soviet Union in 1969.

Even then the dangers of the arms race were well understood,
and the costs were becoming apparent. During the all-encom-
passing strategic nuclear arms race, both the United States and
the Soviet Union built tens of thousands of nuclear weapons
and many thousands of long-range missiles, both land-based and
submarine-based, capable of delivering nuclear weapons with
pinpoint accuracy. In the end, the arms race bankrupted the
Soviet Union, and cost the United States many trillions of dollars. And, if there had been any serious mistakes, world civilization could have been destroyed. To say that things were out
of control is an understatement.

Seeking to bring this reckless and dangerous arms competition under control, in 1969 the Nixon administration began the
first phase of the SALT negotiations. After three years of negotiations between the United States and the Soviet Union, the first
phase of SALT concluded with a treaty limiting strategic defense
(the ABM Treaty) and a companion document called the Interim
Agreement, providing the first limits on strategic offense. Under
the ABM Treaty, each side was limited to two deployments: one
to defend its national capital, and one to defend a single intercontinental ballistic missile deployment field. The treaty was
amended two years later, reducing the permitted anti-ballistic missile deployments to only one. Each side could choose to defend
its national capitol (as the Soviets had done, but a political non-
starter for the Americans) or one intercontinental ballistic missile field (the United States chose this option and elected to defend
its strategic missile deployments at Grand Forks, North Dakota).
The Interim Agreement was a freeze agreement, prohibiting
increased numbers of strategic nuclear weapon systems, leaving
the two sides more or less where they then were, although reflect-

ing a big Soviet buildup that surpassed the large U.S. buildup of previous years.

The United States believed it could tolerate this imbalance because it thought itself far ahead in the technology to put MIRV nuclear warheads, each of which could strike separate targets, on one missile. The United States began placing MIRVs on its strategic missiles in 1970. However, the Soviet Union followed suit as early as 1975, and by the early 1980s, each side had 10,000 to 15,000 nuclear warheads placed on strategic missiles on hair-trigger alert, able to strike the other side thirty minutes after launch, and not recallable once launched. Each country was capable of completely destroying the other many times over. Therefore, although SALT I (the ABM Treaty along with the Interim Agreement) restrained the arms race with respect to building more strategic missiles, the advent of MIRVs spurred it onward. It might have been possible to prohibit MIRVs during the first phase of SALT, but, believing it was far ahead (only five years, as it turned out), the United States did not want to do so.

As appalling as the nuclear arms race became in the late 1970s and early 1980s, the situation would have been far worse if not for SALT. The freeze agreement associated with the first phase of SALT brought the deployment of additional strategic missiles to an end, and the second phase, called the SALT II Treaty (concluded in 1979) took the first steps toward limiting the number of warheads and reducing the number of missiles on each side. Although the SALT II Treaty was not approved by the U.S. Senate, it was informally observed for six years.

The objective of the ABM Treaty, signed in 1972 and from which the United States withdrew in 2002, was, in essence, to prohibit the deployment of large-scale strategic missile defense, thereby making each party vulnerable to attack by the other, a concept known as "assured destruction" or "mutual assured destruction," often referred to by its detractors as "MAD." MAD depended upon the ability of each nation to reply to a nuclear first strike with a massive nuclear weapon response. This meant that both sides had to have sufficient strategic nuclear weapon delivery vehicles so that enough would survive the enemy's initial attack to be able to retaliate in a manner that would incapacitate the enemy. The purpose was to establish crisis stability—to remove any incentive to launch a first strike against the other side. As the basis on which reductions in strategic nuclear forces became possible, it was codified in the ABM Treaty, which obligated strategic defenses to be kept at a very low level. The idea of mutual assured destruction also created arms race stability by removing any incentive for one side to believe it must build more nuclear weapons to overcome defenses being built by the other side. Each party thereby assures the other side of the effectiveness of its strategic nuclear retaliatory forces.

By keeping strategic defense at a low level, the ABM Treaty established the basis for the strategic offensive reductions that are so important for both arms control and crisis stability and for reinforcing the nuclear nonproliferation regime. The ABM Treaty removed the rationale for strategic buildup, but, due to its momentum, the arms race continued for some time. However, the out-of-control arms race of the 1960s would have continued unchecked for years, if not for the stability established by the ABM Treaty, which permitted the negotiation of the later strategic arms reduction treaties of the early 1990s. In their final declaration at the end of their review conference in 2000, the NPT parties rightly referred to the ABM Treaty as the "cornerstone of strategic stability."

In spite of the benefits of peace and stability brought by the ABM Treaty, the dream of absolute security continued to place pressure on the treaty. Secretary Robert McNamara's thin anti-Chinese ballistic missile defense and President Nixon's multi-site safeguard system to defend offensive missile deployments were voided by the ABM Treaty in 1972. However, the United States did construct the one deployment permitted under the treaty: two very large radars, several smaller radars, and 100 ABM interceptor missiles at Grand Forks, North Dakota. This deployment cost $6 billion to build, was completed in 1976, and was closed down after four months of operation, judged too expensive to maintain.

In the 1980s, the issue of missile defense was back—in the form of the Strategic Defense Initiative (SDI) of the 1980s, which aimed to create an "astrodome" in the sky to protect the United States against the now huge Soviet long-range ballistic missile force. The SDI program (or "Star Wars," as it was called by its critics), was based on kinetic "hit-to-kill" interceptors rather than the nuclear-weapon-tipped interceptors that were a feature of the earlier systems. Nuclear-weapon-tipped interceptors had become politically unsustainable, presumably because no one wanted large nuclear explosions in space, and so they remain today. The SDI project was abandoned in the late 1980s, after years of unsuccessful research, as unworkable, impractical, and unnecessary with the waning of the Cold War. By then, however, there was a large industrial infrastructure that supported missile defense, which simply shifted into theater missile defense (defense of U.S. troops and allies overseas against shorter-range missiles), although the technology to be developed was quite robust and could easily have been elevated to strategic ballistic missile defense if it had proved out.

A July 1998 report by the first Rumsfeld Commission (an independent commission funded by the Department of Defense to analyze missile proliferation), spoke of a short-term threat of long-range ballistic missile proliferation to rogue states, and said that the United States could be threatened by such missiles as early as 2005; therefore, it was important to begin building a ballistic missile defense against rogue states. Not highlighted in this argument was the fact that in order to have any degree of reliable capability against the United States, a long-range ballistic missile would require a long series of flight tests, which would give the United States considerable warning time.

Although it may be argued that missile reliability is subject to cultural differences—that North Korea, for example, might not insist on the same degree of accuracy as would the United States before deploying a missile system—in making decisions on expensive defense programs such as missile defense systems, one has to make judgments about the realism of any particular threat. The only type of weapon that it would make sense to use in such an attack with long-range ballistic missiles would be a nuclear weapon. It doesn't make sense to use a long-range ballistic missile to deliver chemical or biological weapons. Chemical weapons have only a very limited area of effectiveness, and the microbes or spores used as biological weapon agents would likely be destroyed upon the impact of the missile carrying them. Developing a nuclear weapon small and light enough to be carried by a ballistic missile the considerable distance from, say, North Korea to the continental United States would almost certainly require a long series of nuclear weapon tests, which would provide additional warning. Nevertheless, missile proliferation is a concern in its own right, and also serves as a rationale for ballistic missile defense.

In 1987, the Missile Technology Control Regime (MTCR) was established to address the threat of ballistic missile proliferation. It is an informal association of approximately thirty-five states who have agreed to control exports of ballistic missiles capable of carrying a 500 kilogram (1,100 pound) payload 300 kilometers (180 miles) and the associated technology, and to coordinate policies to that end. Later it was provided that MTCR would also apply to any missile capable of or intended to carry a WMD warhead 300 kilometers. Unlike the NPT, the Chemical Weapons Convention, and the Biological Weapons Convention, the MTCR is not a treaty. It does not impose limitations and has no verification arrangements. It is strictly an informal technology-control regime. Nevertheless, it has been moderately successful in controlling missile proliferation. To some extent, the ballistic missile proliferation situation has improved. As Professor Dinshaw Mistry of the University of Cincinnati points out in his recent book, *Containing Missile Proliferation* (2003), "Nine regional powers—Argentina, Brazil, South Africa, South Korea, Taiwan, Egypt, Iraq, Syria, and Libya—restrained their ballistic missile efforts in the 1990s. They either ceased missile activity or limited their missile projects to cruise missiles, artillery rockets, and 100–300-kilometer-range [60–180 mile] ballistic missiles. Yet [during the same time frame] five other states—Iran, Pakistan, North Korea, India, and Israel—built and tested 1,000–2,000-kilometer-range [600–1,200 mile] ballistic missiles" (p. 4). The Israeli and Indian medium-range missiles and the medium-range missiles that Saudi Arabia bought from China have solid-fuel rocket engines and possess considerable accuracy. The medium-range missiles of North Korea, Iran, and Pakistan, like the ballistic missiles used by Iran in the first Gulf War, are based on the old Soviet SCUD technology, an advanced version of the V-2 rockets used by Germany in World War II, which had virtually no guidance systems and were large and cumbersome. SCUD missiles are large (and therefore easily targetable), slow, and inaccurate. North Korea did test a three-stage ballistic missile, the Taepodong I, over Japan and into the Pacific, causing worldwide consternation. Nevertheless, the United States is far removed from the range of the medium-range missiles of countries such as Iran and North Korea, and the short-range missiles of Syria are not even a factor. Japan and India do have large space launchers that could be upgraded to intercontinental range, and this is worthy of note.

There is a distant possibility that the North Korean long-range ballistic missile, the Taepodong I, which currently has sufficient range to get about halfway to the continental United States, could be upgraded. But this is problematic in that it would require an extensive test series. This missile has not been tested since 1998. Even by extending its range with a small third stage, it would probably not be capable of carrying any nuclear weapon that North Korea could build in the foreseeable future. No other state is experimenting with long-range or intercontinental ballistic missiles. Thus, there is no foreseeable serious rogue-state long-range ballistic missile threat.

Thus there is no short-term ballistic missile threat against the United States—nor is there likely to be one in the future, except for the two missile threats that have been there for many decades: Russia and China. Russia, for example, has over 1,000 ballistic missiles that could strike the United States (though less than half of what they had during the Cold War). As was concluded after the ending of the SDI program in the 1980s, no conceivable missile defense could be relevant against this force. China has only a small number of intercontinental ballistic missiles—about twenty—but they could easily build more, and could shortly overwhelm, even on paper, any missile defense system now under consideration.

In the late 1990s, an arguably better rationale for missile defense emerged, based on the Rumsfeld Commission report: defense against rogue states. This would be strategic ballistic missile defense, but only against a small number of missiles, and therefore more achievable. After the July 1998 report of the Rumsfeld Commission which had argued that states such as Iran, Iraq, and North Korea might be able to threaten the United States with international ballistic missiles as early as 2005, even some traditional opponents of missile defense came to believe that the threat of missile attack had been underestimated and that something needed to be done. Pursuit of new systems to protect against limited strikes began in the early 1990s and accelerated in the late 1990s, although there was little in the test results to indicate that even this limited system would be practical. While the technology for an effective defense is presently not at hand and may never be, there is a sense among the public that there is no technological challenge the United States cannot overcome.

With the terrible tragedy of the September 11, 2001, attack on the World Trade Center and the Pentagon with highjacked airliners, the political imperative of missile defense became almost irresistible. Some administration spokesmen argued that this attack proved the necessity of missile defense. In mid-September 2001, a senior administration official was reported as saying that "if anything, the likelihood of unilateral withdrawal [from the ABM Treaty] has increased" in the wake of the attacks (*Washington Post*, September 17, 2001). The official went on to say that "these people had jet plane pilots. And if these same people had access to ballistic missiles, do you think they wouldn't have used them?" In the United States, this argument was accepted to a degree, though it is precisely the wrong message to take from the September 11 attacks. The attack was low-tech, not high-tech, and it came with little warning. We would have warning of an incipient long-range missile system threat years in advance, as these large systems require extensive testing and cannot be hidden. Terrorist organizations, the real threat to national security, have never shown the slightest interest in ballistic missiles. Therefore, the message we should have taken from September 11 is that missile attack is an unlikely threat and we should spend our money elsewhere—for example, on intelligence, suppression of terrorist organizations, and similar objectives.

Nevertheless, over the strong objections of our allies, who valued the stability brought by the ABM Treaty, and of the Russians and the Chinese, who feared that their nuclear forces could be nullified by a U.S. missile defense, potentially leaving them at the mercy of U.S. nuclear blackmail, the United States announced on December 13, 2001, that it would withdraw from the ABM Treaty. No member of Congress wanted to face criticism at home that he or she opposed self-defense, and large defense contracts coupled with the attractiveness in principle of defending oneself against "bad guys" created the political situation which led the United States to withdraw from the ABM Treaty in 2002. Subsequently, the United States announced plans to move ahead with an initial missile defense deployment in Alaska of up to twenty ballistic missile interceptors. The deployment in Alaska was declared to be directed toward North Korea, but the number of interceptors matched the number of China's strategic missiles at the time. The present system being deployed in Alaska (and now additionally in California) will have a midcourse intercept mission. Upon warning of a limited attack by a few long-range nuclear missiles from a rogue state, the ground-based interceptor missiles in Alaska, guided by sophisticated sensors in space and on earth, would be launched into space to knock down the incoming warheads. Another theoretical variation would be a boost phase missile defense system that would attempt to destroy the enemy missile during liftoff (the first four or five minutes after launch) from missile defense deployments in space or at sea.

The system that is being deployed in Alaska has a poor test record, and there is no indication it will ever function adequately. On March 11, 2004, the chief of testing and evaluation for the system in the Pentagon, as reported in the *Washington Post* on March 12, 2004, testified before Congress that the system was not sufficiently developed to permit a judgment that it would be effective. Some in the Senate say we should build it whether or not it works, and some in the administration say it could be a kind of "scarecrow." In a sense, we can never know whether a strategic ballistic missile defense system (that is, a defense of the United States against long-range ballistic missiles launched by a hostile state) truly would work in the case of a real attack, because, unlike other weapon systems, it can never be tested in realistic battlefield conditions. Thus, fundamentally, we can never rely upon such a system. Should

North Korea somehow create an accurate international ballistic missile capable of carrying a nuclear warhead to U.S. soil, we will believe ourselves vulnerable with or without a missile defense. On the other hand, the Chinese could "worst-case" our system and decide that their nuclear forces are threatened with being nullified, causing them to significantly increase the size of their long-range nuclear missile force—up to ten times, in their own words—thereby worsening the threat to the United States.

There appears little to be gained by a missile defense on which we can never fully rely, and much to be lost in terms of reducing our focus on the real threat and increasing forces amassed against us. Ten billion dollars is the funding request for the missile defense program for fiscal year 2005—the largest single-year expenditure ever on a weapon system. In sum, the United States has spent somewhere in the range of $100 billion on ballistic missile defense at no increase (and perhaps some decrease) to its security.

In this age of the war on terror, the United States is vulnerable not to sophisticated ballistic missile systems that leave an easily recognizable return address but rather to the demonic use of relatively unsophisticated or crude weapons by hidden and anonymous opponents determined to undermine our way of life. Terrorists or rogue states delivering weapons of mass destruction—particularly nuclear weapons—by long-range ballistic missiles is one of the least likely threats that we face. To paraphrase a statement made by former Senator Daniel Patrick Moynihan several years ago, to focus on missile defenses in the era of international terrorism at the expense of addressing the threat of clandestine weapons brought into the United States by stealth is the equivalent of "shooting above the target." In this day and age, it is important to shoot straight.

8

Outer Space

DECEMBER 1, 2003, MARKED THE FORTY-FOURTH anniversary of the signing of the first arms control agreement of the modern era, the Antarctic Treaty, which preserved the continent as a nonmilitarized, nuclear-weapon-free area. The debate that preceded the negotiation of that treaty is remarkably similar to contemporary discussion on the future of outer space. In the early to mid-1950s, there were approximately a dozen countries vying for scientific, economic, and military interests in Antarctica—an uninhabited, borderless, and lawless land. In time, and after much debate, twelve states (with others joining afterward) decided that the greater interests of all of the affected parties would best be served if the continent could be preserved for peaceful uses, and that those interests could best be protected through a legal arrangement rather than through the use or deployment of military forces. Thus, the Antarctic Treaty was signed on December 1, 1959.

The international community is now faced with protecting

the opportunities and assets associated with the use of outer space. Here again we have a borderless realm rich in commercial, scientific, and military potential, and questions about how best to preserve those critical assets. Will military deployments and the weaponization of space be required? Is (as some have suggested) the weaponization of space an inevitable evolution of current and historical realities? Or is it possible, or even desirable, to instead craft a legal arrangement preserving space as a peaceful realm? Perhaps a third way will present itself. For example, could there be some combination of approaches whereby both legal restraints and militarization are part of the equation? These are but a few of the questions facing those working to protect access to space.

A great deal rides on the answers to these questions. Scientifically, the stakes are quite high—everything from the International Space Station to the Hubble Space Telescope and the exploration of Mars would potentially be affected by instability and unpredictability in outer space. The commercial implications are even greater. For example, in *Foreign Affairs* magazine several years ago, Michael Krepon estimated that space-technology industries generated $125 billion in profits in 2000; by 2010, the cumulative U.S. investment in space is expected to reach as high as $600 billion—roughly the equivalent of the total current U.S. investment in Europe ("Lost in Space," May-June, 2001, p. 5). Even with a less favorable economic climate, as in 2003, the commercial stakes are high. Clearly, it is now more important than ever to protect space assets.

It is also evident that outer space is becoming a more dangerous place. Several countries—including Russia, the United States, and perhaps China—have had programs to develop sophisticated anti-satellite weapons, and several others are thought to be seeking such technologies. If anti-satellite weapons continue to proliferate, they have the potential to dramatically undermine fundamental U.S. interests, including national security and international commerce. Krepon cites, for example, that a May 1998 failure by a single Galaxy IV satellite caused 80 percent of the pagers in America to go dead, affecting some 27 million users. A realization of the increasing vulnerability of the United States to attacks against space assets has caused some to encourage Washington to begin deploying defensive weapon systems. Although this appears to make sense, a thoughtful analysis of the history of military development reveals flaws with this notion. Most importantly, modern history categorically demonstrates that effective defensive weapon systems will inevitably be countered by effective offensive systems, sparking an ever-upward-spiraling arms race that ultimately leaves all sides less secure.

For supporting evidence, one need look no further than the second half of the twentieth century and the nuclear arms race that dominated it. Until the United States and the Soviet Union signed the ABM Treaty in 1972, effectively preventing each side from deploying defensive systems, the nuclear weapon competition between the two superpowers was constantly threatening to escalate out of control. For the same reason, the international community of space-faring nations should recognize the need for restraint and seek to develop some legal regime to preserve outer space as a non-weaponized realm. It is important that this happen as soon as possible; most nations already consider the possibility of weapons being deployed in space as highly threatening to their security. The Canadian government has unequivocally stated that it "draws the line at weapons in space." In mid-2003, both Canada and Russia agreed to cooperate with the United States on ballistic missile defense, on the condition that no ballistic missile defense weapons be placed in space.

The legal basis for a regime that preserves space as a non-weaponized realm may already exist. Indeed, international law (including efforts to control weapons) is no stranger to the space environment. The Outer Space Treaty, signed in 1967, bans the deployment of nuclear weapons and any other weapons of mass destruction in Earth orbit, or in orbit around any celestial body, or elsewhere in space. It also limits the use of the moon and other celestial bodies to peaceful purposes. The Antarctic Treaty, the Outer Space Treaty, and later the 1972 Seabed Arms Control Treaty, which prohibited the deployment of weapons of mass destruction on the ocean floor and in the subsoil thereof, are in a unique class of arms control agreements sometimes referred to as "nonarmament treaties" (as discussed in Chapter 3). These agreements were intended to and have been successful at preventing the deployment of nuclear weapons in areas where they had not previously been present. Today, after more than three decades, the Antarctic, space, and the ocean floor all remain free of weapons of mass destruction. As mentioned in Chapter 3, space has long been militarized with the deployment of military reconnaissance and navigation satellites and similar technologies. However, no offensive or defensive weapons have ever been stationed in outer space. It has been suggested that a legal regime to prevent the weaponization of space could be crafted by simply expanding or building upon the Outer Space Treaty. Considering the fact that the Outer Space Treaty has more than ninety states parties, there may be some merit to the notion of amending it to ban weaponization.

A crucial reason to seek a non-weaponized space environment is the need to protect satellites and other space-based assets used to collect intelligence and to ensure verification of compliance with many international treaties limiting armaments (often referred to as national technical means of verification). Such space assets have been used to verify compliance with international security treaties and enhance international peace and security for nearly four decades. As part of its limitation of the deployment of national missile defense systems by the United States and Russia, the ABM Treaty prohibited the development, testing and

deployment of space-based interceptors. The ABM Treaty also prohibited interference by either party with the other's monitoring
satellites. The START Treaty contains the same provision, as does
the Treaty on Conventional Armed Forces in Europe.

Because of the central role they generally play in preserving
confidence in the nonproliferation regime and in international
security arrangements, ensuring noninterference with space
assets is crucial to ensuring peace and security for the twenty-first
century. President Ronald Reagan's devotion to the Russian
adage "trust but verify" was absolutely correct. Without space-
based national technical means, international security would be
virtually impossible—a reality of which U.S. and Russian nego-
tiators have been keenly aware during the arms control and international security negotiations of the past thirty years.

Such considerations apply not only in the bilateral U.S.-
Russian context but also to the broad range of international security accords. For example, activities detected through space-
based national technical means can be used to trigger requests for
on-site inspections pursuant to the Chemical Weapons Convention or the Comprehensive Nuclear-Test-Ban Treaty (should the
latter be brought into force). It is important to recall that suspi-
cions that Israel and South Africa may have conducted an atmospheric nuclear test in the South Atlantic during the late 1970s were
driven by disputed readouts from an American Vela satellite.

At present, satellite imagery is regularly used to track activities that could reveal programs to develop weapons of mass
destruction in countries of concern around the world. These are
crucial efforts that we must never allow to be disrupted—especially
not while relatively simplistic weapons systems still exist that could
someday be deployed to counter anti-satellite weapon defense systems. Given the relentless progression of technological development, ensuring that these monitoring and verification measures
are protected is an objective that can probably ultimately be

achieved only through an international agreement entered into by the entire world community.

There are, of course, many other highly important interests to protect in space, such as remote sensing, telecommunications, and navigation systems. Active defenses (the deployment of devices intended to deflect, destroy, or render unworkable offensive weapons) cannot by themselves be expected to provide adequate protection of these space assets in the long term. Already, China has apparently claimed to have developed tiny parasitic satellites that float through space and discreetly attach themselves to larger satellites. Once attached, their purpose would be to hang around like barnacles on the underside of a boat, await instructions from remote operators on earth, and detonate on command. This is only the beginning of what, if left unchecked, is likely to become an inexorable progression in capabilities. Some way to defend against the current generation of anti-satellite technology may very well be found, but our would-be attackers will certainly find ways to counter those defenses.

Additionally, the exclusive character of the current space security regime could weaken its effectiveness in the future. Currently, the international arrangement that most directly addresses this issue is the MTCR. As described in the previous chapter, it is a voluntary arrangement among the world's dominant technological actors, intended to restrict the proliferation of missiles and related technology. While primarily directed toward ballistic missiles, technically it can apply to cruise missiles as well.

Although the MTCR has achieved limited success in stemming the spread of missile technology, it has also had the effect of inhibiting the development of some nations' peaceful space programs. Given the fact that the importance of space technology for national security applications, scientific advancement, and a nation's ability to compete economically will only increase in the twenty-first century, it is no wonder that an increasing number of states perceive the pursuit of space capabilities to be of vital national interest.

As more nations set their sights on the rewards offered by developing their own indigenous space programs, the prospect of the proliferation of space technology over the last decade has caused alarm among some security policy makers. The main source of the concern is that the same technology that allows humankind to reach and subsequently utilize space can also be used for weapons-related purposes. The space-based elements of President Reagan's Strategic Defense Initiative program in the 1980s were the core of Soviet objections to the program because if that program had proceeded to development, it would have been in violation of the ABM Treaty. Although it is a difficult task to find a reasonable balance between upholding the principle of universal space access and preventing the application of dual-use technology for harmful purposes, it is nevertheless crucial for maintaining a sustainable security regime.

Ballistic missiles are not the only potentially harmful application of dual-use space technology. For example, space platforms for scientific or commercial uses could be converted into orbital weapons carriers, and any object in space with sufficient maneuverability can be used as a kinetic energy weapon (destroyed by collision). It is unlikely that the MTCR is comprehensive enough to confront future contingencies of this nature, and likely there will be considerations of further measures that could be undertaken as part of a long-term solution.

Shutter control (limiting the utilization of particular remote-sensing space assets in certain areas) has been considered in the past, but such an approach to information management could be outdated. Today, it would be very difficult for the U.S. government to impose shutter control on all remote-sensing companies, since there are so many more of them than there were in early 1990s, both at home and abroad. Exercising leverage over foreign companies would involve leaning on foreign governments, which could cost considerable time and money. In addition, news media in the United States are poised for a First Amendment fight if they are denied the right to purchase satellite imagery.

The greater part of the international community will not accept a security regime which is built upon the principles of enforced technological denial and which does not recognize the right of all nations to engage in this pursuit. Any new behavioral criteria, transparency guidelines, monitoring procedures, or methods of enforcement adopted to promote greater space security will thus obtain high levels of compliance only if they are perceived to be legitimate and consistent with the interests of all parties. Therefore, a legal regime predicated upon mutually beneficial and, of course, verifiable restraint should be developed. Otherwise, the world can expect that a significant number of nations who see greater security benefits in defiance rather than in cooperation will continually challenge the viability of the future space security framework.

The very nature of orbiting suggests numerous ways that users around the globe can cooperate, exchanging civilian, space exploration, education, military, and commercial information. The simplest level of cooperation includes data exchange on weather, remote sensing, and radiation monitoring. The mutual benefits to be reaped would include cost sharing, political incentives, and enlargement of the ground infrastructure network. Telecommunications, remote sensing, and satellite-based navigation systems are all commercially available space applications that have dual-use potential. Some of the military applications, such as reconnaissance and navigation satellites, have already been mentioned. The International Space Station is one example of international cooperation in space exploration.

The world's militaries have an interest in such applications, and acquisition of these capabilities by a terrorist organization or national adversary could have serious implications for U.S. military operations. The maintenance of some U.S. military control over access to such global utilities as commercial remote sensing satellites could be justified in instances such as the one during the 1991 Gulf War, when U.S. coalition forces performed a "left hook" maneuver that would have been severely compromised had it been detected early on by the opposition through remote sensing capabilities. Or an enemy's gaining knowledge of where Patriot missile batteries are deployed might increase the missile threat for civilian and U.S. military targets. These examples could take place in the context of a battle or war, but there are also scenarios that may occur outside of a wartime situation. For example, terrorist groups might be able to develop capabilities that use the Global Positioning System (GPS) for targeting an attack; e.g., an unmanned version of the attack perpetrated against the USS *Cole*, in which terrorists drove a small boat laden with explosives into the side of a U.S. navy ship anchored in a harbor in Yemen.

In other cases, military control over access to global utilities could be unattainable. For example, remote-sensing companies in the United States are not allowed to sell imagery of the island of Diego Garcia in the Indian Ocean, since it is the home of a U.S. military base. Recently, a customer in India who wanted to purchase satellite photos of the island approached a U.S. company. In order to cover themselves, the U.S. company simply asked an Israeli company to provide the image. Thus, while the U.S. government can have some influence on the behavior of domestic and foreign imaging entities, the cost of doing so can be politically high, in that an appeal might have to be made to a foreign government to discipline one if its own companies when, under their laws, nothing improper had been done.

The inexorable improvement and dissemination of technology on the one hand, and the increasing inability of the U.S. government to maintain high levels of control over the use of commercial space systems—particularly remote sensing—on the other, suggest that U.S. security in space cannot be maintained over the long run, either by defensive weapons or by unilateral political control. This argues for a strong commitment to international space cooperation and the gradual development of a comprehensive international legal regime for outer space. The groundwork for such a comprehensive treaty-based regime has been laid. Much work remains, but the creation of a space regime under which the international community decisively enshrines space as a peaceful environment is the only thoroughgoing alternative to a weaponized space free-for-all in which the United States and the rest of the world are rendered forever vulnerable to the vagaries and fluctuations of technological development and political instability.

9

Cleaning Up
After Past Wars:
Land Mines and
Small Arms

THE COLD WAR PRESENTED THE WORLD WITH A
litany of potential disasters, cost trillions of dollars in pre-
cious national resources, and left much danger and potential
destruction in its wake, including vast arsenals of nuclear weapons,
other weapons of mass destruction, and related materials. The
antipersonnel land mines and countless small arms left behind
also pose an increasing threat to humanity.

An estimated 100 million antipersonnel land mines are still
deployed in various countries—many where they can no longer
be identified. An antipersonnel land mine is a mine designed
to kill a human being and which can be detonated by the pressure applied by stepping on it. In post-conflict societies, it is most
often the civilian going about his or her daily activities who
becomes the unfortunate victim of a land mine. Up to 25,000
people a year are killed by encountering one of them. A land

mine cannot distinguish between soldiers and civilians; it will kill or maim a child playing football just as readily as a soldier on patrol. Mines have frequently been used in deliberate and systematic wars against civilians, especially in the bitter internal conflicts that came to characterize warfare in the late twentieth century, of which Bosnia, Lebanon, Afghanistan, and Cambodia are examples. These tragic realities make the antipersonnel land mine a particularly abhorrent weapon.

At the first Review Conference for the Convention on Certain Conventional Weapons (CCW) in 1996 (as discussed in Chapter 3), the parties, after several attempts, were unable to reach a consensus on how to deal with the global land mine problem. Protocol 2 of the convention introduced useful changes to limits on mine warfare, but fell short of a total ban on antipersonnel land mines—a move already supported by more than forty countries. Protocol 2 was amended at the Review Conference in 1996, but the attempt to convert it into a complete ban on antipersonnel land mines failed. At the end of the conference, the Canadian delegation announced a meeting of states supporting a ban on antipersonnel mines to be held in Ottawa later that year with the objective of developing a strategy for moving the international community forward. This was the beginning of what became known as the Ottawa Process.

After the failure to effectively amend Protocol 2, the designated International Strategy Conference was held in October 1996 in Ottawa, at the end of which Canadian Foreign Minister Lloyd Axworthy appealed to all governments to return to Ottawa at the end of 1997 to sign a treaty banning antipersonnel land mines. His initiative was immediately supported by the International Committee of the Red Cross, the International Campaign to Ban Landmines, and the UN secretary-general. A few weeks later, the Austrian government circulated a draft treaty that prohibited the production, stockpiling, transfer, and use of antipersonnel land mines; called for the destruction of stockpiles in one year; and called for the clearance of emplaced mines in five years. In December 1996, the UN General Assembly supported the effort to ban land mines by a vote of 157 in favor, with 10 abstentions. This was followed by a series of diplomatic meetings which led to a conference in Oslo, Norway, the following September.

The Oslo Conference was preceded by a conference in Brussels, Belgium, at which 97 countries agreed to the basic elements of a land mine treaty: a comprehensive ban on the use, stockpiling, production, and transfer of antipersonnel mines; the destruction of all cleared antipersonnel land mines; and international cooperation and assistance in clearing mines in affected countries.

The Olso Conference began on September 1, 1997. Only the 97 states that had signed the Brussels Declaration containing the agreed basic elements of a land mine treaty were entitled to vote; all others were classified as observers. The rules of procedure provided for a two-thirds vote to resolve issues if consensus could not be achieved. With skill and determination, the conference chairman, Ambassador Jacob Selebi of South Africa, drove the process, and agreement was reached in less than the allotted three weeks. On September 18, the conference formally adopted the Convention on the Prohibition of the Use, Stockpiling, Production, and Transfer of Antipersonnel Mines and on Their Destruction, which became known as the Ottawa Convention.

During the Oslo negotiations, the United States had sought an exemption for U.S. deployments in South Korea, given the political-military situation on the Korean Peninsula, as well as for antipersonnel land mines deployed to protect anti-tank mines (anti-tank and anti-vehicle mines are regulated by the CCW). Both proposals were rejected by the conference, after which the United States decided not to sign, although it pledged to seek alternatives to its two requested exemptions to permit it to eventually join and to assist in mine clearance worldwide.

The Ottawa Convention was opened for signature on December 3, 1997, and entered into force upon the deposit of the fortieth ratification on March 1, 1999. By April 2004, 150 nations had signed the convention and 141 countries (including six direct accessions without signing) had ratified or acceded to the convention and thereby become parties. The Ottawa Convention is an important first step in dealing with this scourge, but the process will not be complete until Russia, China, and the United States can see their way clear to joining this important treaty designed to make the world safe for civilians living in former war zones.

Also of serious concern in the wake of the Cold War is the spread of dangerous small arms around the world, referred to in diplomatic discussions as "small arms and light weapons," which includes weapons such as assault rifles, machine guns, and grenade launchers. These weapons kill an estimated 100,000 people a year in the many small wars around the globe. Access to these weapons has become easier and more widespread, including both international transfer and transfer within states. The elimination of large-scale illegal production and transfer of such weapons, coupled with establishment of global norms should be an objective.

During my travels in support of indefinite extension of the NPT, many of my interlocutors from countries around the world stressed the importance of curtailing the international illegal transfer of small arms. Often they would say, "We agree with you about the importance of a permanent NPT, now let us talk about what is of greatest concern to us." They identified the diffusion of small arms as a threat to their national security in the same way that the United States views the proliferation of weapons of mass destruction as a threat to its national security. Illegal transfers of weapons have become a security concern for an increasing number of countries.

In South Africa, illegal import and export of conventional weapons is a central security concern. In Mexico, a flood of illegal weapons from the United States is closely associated with the drug trade, and serves as an impetus to widespread lawlessness. Peru has been deeply concerned with this issue, given the continuing supply of small arms to local terrorist organizations. Norway has made a useful proposal for curtailing indiscriminate weapons transfers.

But key supplier states, such as the United States, Russia, and China, are not as quick to identify the problem as a threat to their own security interests. This is a shortsighted view. In the United States, for instance, more than 30,000 people die every year from firearm-related injuries. In light of the steady stream of tragedies occurring within our own country every day, it is incomprehensible to many around the world that the United States is not more proactive in controlling small arms. However, many countries recognize that it is important to the success of effective international small arms control that it be kept entirely separate from the internal situation in the United States.

It is urgent for the world community to develop criteria for determining which types of small arms may legitimately be part of international commerce. For example, there is no justification for items such as AK-47 assault rifles ever to be part of international trade, unless destined for recipients such as military establishments. Even more important is the need for more international cooperation to retard illegal trade in weapons.

Arms control can be defined as an effort to establish negotiated limits, reductions, controls, or prohibitions on the development, testing, deployment, or use of weapons or weapons systems or essential related component materials. Modern arms control has focused primarily on limiting weapons that destabilize the military balance of power among states. However, the lessons learned from the arms control process of the past could open doors for employing arms control to achieve other objectives, such as controlling small arms.

First, the signing of the landmine treaty demonstrated the impact that civil society—and nongovernmental organizations in particular—can have in promoting legal restraints on the spread of weapons. The Ottawa Process leading to the landmine treaty was for a long time led by nongovernmental organizations— both before and after governments became involved. And it is a commonly understood characteristic of arms control agreements that total bans are more readily enforceable than quantitative limits. This was taken into account in the Ottawa negotiations. In the case of small arms control, it may be useful to treat the implementation of agreements as a hybrid of arms control and law enforcement.

The second lesson that we can learn from traditional arms control is that verification and enforcement play an important role in keeping treaty compliance in the interest of all parties by raising the potential costs of violation. Increased international cooperation in these areas holds considerable promise, but with regard to agreements limiting small arms traffic, a high degree of effectiveness in verification and enforcement may be much more difficult to achieve than with regard to treaties that limit, for example, strategic weapons. Individual weapons may be difficult to control; however, this does not mean that we should walk away from arms control. Perfect enforcement may not be nearly so important if an individual treaty violation has no major impact on society. With nuclear arms control, 99 percent confidence that your opponent is not cheating is often not considered sufficient. However, 50 percent confidence that an opponent is not employing small arms may still be beneficial to both sides. Even an imperfect treaty regime limiting such weapons may lessen the destructiveness of a conflict.

The third lesson to be learned from traditional arms control is that in endeavoring to control any type of weapon, it is often important to realize that the weapon itself may not be the most viable target of effective arms control. For example, in the case of chemical weapons, the focus should be not only on complete weapons but also on the precursor chemicals that can be used in their manufacture. This may be a useful approach for small arms; for example, restriction of access to ammunition may limit the destructiveness of weapons already in dangerous hands. Export controls are becoming more and more critical to controlling dangerous materials and technologies. The kind of enhanced international cooperation, national legislation, and local implementation programs that many countries are engaged in to control nuclear, chemical, biological, missile, and precision-guidance technologies could readily be extended to cover small arms and ammunition. However, major exporters, such as the United States, Russia, and China, must be involved if such controls are to be effective.

And the fourth and perhaps most important lesson traditional arms control offers for limiting small arms traffic is to not give up on a good idea just because it is difficult. For decades, a negotiated end to the superpower nuclear arms race seemed impossible, and now the United States and Russia are working to dismantle nuclear weapons. No one could have predicted the changes in the international political environment of the last ten years, and there is no reason to believe that the next ten years will be any more predictable. Imagination and perseverance will lead us to future opportunities that no one can now anticipate.

Only treaties that are in the interest of all parties can be negotiated, and only treaties that remain in the interest of all parties will be honored. Effective arms control is cooperative arms control. It is essential to remember that arms limitation is not an end in itself; it is not a moral good, as is peace. Arms control is, at its best, an important component of national security policy in the modern age. A treaty will not take away the malice in men's hearts, but it can afford us the opportunity to define unacceptable behavior and to threaten the perpetrators of such behavior with severe consequences.

The world community must move toward the establishment of a tighter and tighter web of interlocking legal regimes serving to reinforce one other by raising the price of violation of any of the international norms they embody. The rule of law among sovereign states means more today than it ever has in history, and its importance is steadily increasing. Treaties are not scripture. Academic debates that insist that a treaty is useless unless it is perfect are counterproductive. The quest for perfection must not be an obstacle to this common goal when human life and suffering are at stake.

10

Poison Gas
and Microbes:
Chemical and
Biological Weapons

I N 1899, AT THE INVITATION OF CZAR NICHOLAS II
of Russia, an international peace conference was convened
at The Hague in the Netherlands. The purpose of the conference was to limit the ever-growing destructive power of weapons
of war. This conference concluded with a declaration which,
among other things, outlawed the use of asphyxiating gas in warfare. A follow-on conference held at The Hague in 1907 prohibited poisoned weapons. Thus poison gas was internationally
outlawed prior to World War I. Unfortunately, this did not prevent the use of poison gas in that war, as the Hague declarations
were ignored by the combatants. On April 22, 1915, near Ypres,
Belgium, German troops dispensed an estimated 150 tons of chlorine gas from thousands of cylinders (as reported in Chapter 3 of
the *U.S. Armed Forces Nuclear Biological and Chemical Survival
Manual*, 2003). The wind blew the gas over the Allied trenches,
causing more than 5,000 casualties among the Allied troops. Later,
the Allies retaliated with a chlorine gas attack of their own. After

some time, both sides developed masks that offered complete protection against chlorine and other poison gases that worked by
inhalation. The manual cites a passage from the poem "Dulce
et Decorum Est" by the British poet Wilfred Owen, describing
what a gas attack was like in those years:

> Gas! GAS! Quick, boys!—An ecstasy of fumbling,
> Fitting the clumsy helmets just in time;
> But someone still was yelling out and stumbling
> And floundering like a man in fire or lime.—
> Dim, through the misty panes and thick green light
> As under a green sea, I saw him drowning.
>
> In all my dreams, before my helpless sight,
> He plunges at me, guttering, choking, drowning.

In 1917, the German army introduced a new type of poison
gas, a blistering agent known as "mustard gas." It was highly toxic,
and its first use in an attack resulted in 20,000 Allied casualties.
During the rest of the war, mustard gas was used extensively by
both sides; it alone produced some 400,000 casualties, making
it the greatest casualty producer of the last years of World War I.
In order to be safe from mustard gas, the entire body had to be
protected. Before the war was over, poison gas had caused some
100,000 deaths and more than one million often-crippling casualties. New types of poison gases were developed in the years leading up to World War II—in particular, the deadly nerve agents
which kill very quickly with just a drop on the skin. Nerve agents
such as tabun and sarin, originally developed by Germany, were
used along with mustard gas by Iraqi forces against the Iranians
in the 1980s and are now widespread.

The public came to regard poison gas as a particularly despi-
cable weapon, which led to serious efforts to prohibit it in the
1920s. There were several attempts to convene an international

conference on chemical weapons in the years immediately following World War I, but they were not successful until, in 1925,
on the margins of a conference on the international arms trade
in Geneva, Switzerland, an agreement afterwards known as the
Geneva Protocol was concluded, banning the use in war of chemical (poison gas) weapons, and, as an afterthought, of bacteriological (biological) weapons. As a rule on the conduct of warfare
rather than an arms control agreement, it does not contain verification provisions. Because of reservations adopted by many parties
upon ratification, the Geneva Protocol is, in effect, an agreement
prohibiting parties to the protocol from the first use in war of chemical and biological weapons. For example, France's reservation,
adopted after its legislature approved the protocol for ratification,
provides that France's obligations under the protocol apply only
among parties to the protocol, and that France is released from
its obligations with respect to any enemy state whose armed forces
do not observe the provisions of the protocol.

By the 1930s, most of the major world powers had ratified the
protocol, but the United States did not do so until 1975. Nevertheless, in 1943, in the middle of World War II, President Franklin
Delano Roosevelt announced that the United States would never
be the first to use these weapons, and that the use of chemical and
biological weapons had been "outlawed by the general opinion
of civilized mankind," or in other words by customary international
law. Thus, the provisions of the protocol, because of long and widespread acceptance, are considered to be part of international law
binding on all states whether or not they are parties to the protocol, the violation of which can be the basis of a war crime charge.

Chemical or poison gas weapons were not used in World War
II, and there have been only a few instances of violations of the
Geneva Protocol since its signature in 1925. Italy used chemical
weapons in Ethiopia in 1935, and Egypt used them in Yemen in
1967, but the most flagrant use was during the Iran-Iraq war of

the 1980s. Iraq had begun the war in an attempt to seize Iranian oil fields in the south. Poison gas weapons were used initially by Iraq in a limited fashion, which gradually escalated to massive use by the later stages of the war. Iran responded in kind, but in a lesser degree. There were thousands of casualties and, over time, military action became stalemated. Toward the end of the war, Iraq prevented defeat by extensive use of chemical weapons against unprotected Iranian citizen soldiers.

Biological weapons go further back in history than chemical weapons. In the fifteenth century, the Spanish in Peru presented the natives with clothing contaminated by smallpox, which spread rapidly and decimated the Indian population. The British did the same thing in 1759, during the French and Indian War, with devastating results for the opposing Indian forces. During World War II, however, only the Japanese (who did not ratify the Geneva Protocol until 1970) employed biological weapons—and that on only a limited basis, against China. Japan experimented with anthrax as a biological weapon during World War II, and by 1945 had produced 800 pounds of anthrax spores, which can be used in fragmentation bombs and which produce a highly lethal respiratory infection. In 1990, shortly before the first Gulf War, Iraq had filled a number of deliverable weapons with anthrax spores as well as botulinum toxin, an extremely toxic chemical produced by the bacterium Clostridium botulinum, which causes the deadly illness known as botulism.

The Geneva Protocol did not address the question of national stockpiles of chemical and biological weapons such as Iraq possessed before the first Gulf War in 1991, however. Stockpiles that exist may tempt their use, and they and their chemical ingredients are always subject to the threat of acquisition by terrorist organizations. The Geneva Protocol also does not address the question of the use of chemical and biological weapons by terrorist organizations and other subnational groups or by governments against their own populations, such as the poison gas attack by the Iraqi army on Iraq's Kurdish minority in 1988. Although the possibility of the use of chemical or biological weapons in war still exists, the probability is low. Officials of a state that violates the protocol today become liable for war crimes charges. Of course, subnational or extra-national terrorist organizations would not be influenced by the Geneva Protocol or customary international law. They are essentially international criminals who must be dealt with by a united world community upholding the rule of law.

On March 20, 1995, Aum Shinrikyo, a Japanese cult bent on destruction, released sarin gas on the Tokyo subway system. The following is a passage from *Holy Terror* by D. W. Brackett (1996, p. 3), a book which chronicles this attack and the events leading up to it:

> Some thirty passengers have detrained in a crush, handkerchiefs pressed to their eyes and mouths as they flee toward the station exits. Screams of "Help!" and "I can't see!" echo from the platforms and down the warm corridors of the station where dazed passengers sink to their knees in agony and fear, unable to understand what is happening to them, and why their bodies do not function properly.
>
> The first stricken passengers to climb out of the station depths to street level are now making their appearance outside the Kamiyacho Station entrance. But the fresh winter air filling their lungs brings no relief, and those most heavily exposed to the fumes take only a few steps before collapsing in a heap on the sidewalk. Others are bent double in agony; everyone who had been below is pale. Many are vomiting and several people are frothing at the mouth, their eyes open, but unseeing, as they are carried away on stretchers. Others lie prostrate on the concrete streets, some receiving heart massages from passers-by who mistake them for heart-attack victims.
>
> "I was in the car when suddenly there was a smell like paint

thinner," a twenty-eight-year-old company worker from the Meguro Ward neighborhood in Tokyo later said, "the next moment my eyes ceased to focus, and I lost my vision. What happened?"

The potential for seriously damaging effects from terrorist use of chemical or biological weapons is a realistic threat that cannot be discounted. Chemical weapons are serious weapons of war, but weapons against which well-trained and well-equipped troops can nevertheless fully protect themselves. Civilians, however, will ordinarily not be protected. Many thousands of Kurdish villagers were killed by poison gas attacks conducted by the Iraqi Army in the late 1980s. It has been said that if the Japanese terrorists had used a higher concentration of sarin gas in the Tokyo subway system than they did that March morning (for example, a 70-80 percent pure mixture, rather than the 30 percent pure mixture that was used) instead of 12 deaths and 5,000 injuries, there could have been up to 25,000 deaths and enormous numbers of casualties.

Unlike chemical weapons, biological weapons are not particularly useful as battlefield weapons. To spray an oncoming force with an agent that will make them sick several days later is unlikely to diminish the vigor of their attack. However, the strategic use of biological agents such as anthrax, plague, or smallpox could be a threat to civilian populations—all the more so in the case of an unanticipated terrorist attack. A small number of anthrax-tainted letters that were mailed in the United States in the fall of 2001 caused widespread evacuation of government offices and crippled the postal system for some months. Epidemics caused by the use of such weapons against civilian populations by states or by terrorist groups could likely be contained in first world countries with modern public health systems, with significant, but not overwhelming damage. In third world countries, however, the effects could be devastating.

The world community long ago concluded that chemical and biological weapons should be delegitimized and outlawed. The first step was the Geneva Protocol, in effect prohibiting their first use in war. The second step was the negotiation of the Biological Weapons Convention, which became effective in 1975. The convention outlawed these weapons and prohibited their use and even their possession "in any circumstances." Thus, a response to an attack by biological weapons must be with force involving other types of weapons. Biological weapons are easy to make, but if they are barred from the arsenals of states and outlawed by a united world community, it will be more difficult for international terrorist organizations to make and use them. Unfortunately, the Biological Weapons Convention treaty has no verification provisions, and toward the end of the Cold War it was discovered that the Soviet Union had been cheating on a massive scale. The vast illegal Soviet bioweapon infrastructure has been dismantled by Russia, but, of course, the capability in terms of scientific expertise remains. Efforts have been undertaken by the United States to provide their scientists with peaceful commercial opportunities.

The third step toward limiting chemical and biological weapons was the negotiation of the Chemical Weapons Convention in 1993 and its entry into force in 1997. This treaty followed the basic outline of the Biological Weapons Convention, but went much further. It delegitimized and outlawed poison gas weapons, and prohibited their use and possession "in any circumstances" as well. But it also set forth detailed schedules of prohibited chemicals and established a highly intrusive and complex on-site inspection and verification system. It may be easy to manufacture chemical weapons, but it will be difficult for any country that joins this treaty to make them in militarily significant quantities without eventually being detected by the comprehensive verification regime. Approximately 150 countries have joined the

Chemical Convention to date, making it increasingly unlikely that poison gas weapons will ever again be used in war, and greatly strengthening the hand of the world community against the possibility of terrorist acquisition and use of these weapons.

The fourth step has been the attempt to develop an inspection and verification system for the Biological Weapons Convention like that of the Chemical Weapons Convention. Negotiations began in the mid-1990s, and over some seven years, considerable progress was made toward this objective. A less-than-perfect but nevertheless important move forward was to be completed in 2002 in the form of an inspection protocol to the Biological Weapons Convention. It would have provided for an inspection regime for biological weapons that would have made it more difficult for states belonging to the treaty to secretly possess biological weapons. As with the Chemical Weapons Convention, it would have strengthened the hand of the world community against possible terrorist possession and use of the weapons. Unfortunately, at the very last moment, the United States had serious questions as to the effectiveness of the protocol in preventing proliferation of biological weapons. U.S. biotech companies were complaining about the contemplated on-site inspection process. The United States decided to block agreement on the inspection protocol, and, instead of offering an alternative document, elected to destroy the entire negotiation process. Objecting to the protocol in its then-existing form was understandable, but the destruction of the process was inexplicable. Let us hope that this decision will be reversed and that a strong and effective inspection arrangement for biological weapons can be developed, so as to reduce the risk that these horrible weapons will ever again be used, by states or by terrorists.

11

Controlling
Nuclear Materials:
The Situation
in Russia

D ESPITE THE END OF THE COLD WAR, NUCLEAR weapons still pose a devastating threat to the United States and to the world community. The risk of thermonuclear war between the two superpowers has faded, but has been replaced by a much higher risk that a major city or several major cities could be destroyed by stealth by a rogue state or a terrorist organization. The vast oversupply of nuclear weapons and nuclear explosive material left over from the Cold War is not protected nearly as well as it was in the closed society of the former Soviet Union, or as well as it should be. It potentially represents a dagger pointed at the heart of the United States and the civilized world.

The Soviet Union was a closed society, and with closed borders and a large well-compensated corps of scientists it built a most effective security system for its nuclear stockpile. But this system vanished with the Soviet Union, and now there are a dozen states with open borders, limited nuclear export controls, and desperately underpaid or even unpaid scientists and guards. The following is an excerpt from a report published by the Center for Strategic and International Studies of Washington in January 2000 (*Managing the Global Nuclear Material Threat, Policy Recommendations*, p. 15):

> Nuclear guards reportedly go unpaid for months at a time and leave their posts to forage for food; nuclear security systems go unmaintained or even unused for lack of funds; electricity that provides the lifeblood of nuclear alarm and monitoring systems is shut off for nonpayment of bills; and in several documented cases, kilogram quantities of weapons-usable nuclear material are stolen. . . . the Russian Minister of Atomic Energy has acknowledged that the reduction in Russia's ability to control nuclear materials is "immeasurable." The Central Intelligence Agency has gone further, warning that the risk that potential bomb materials could fall into the hands of terrorists and proliferant states is higher than ever before.

By purchasing or stealing a relatively small amount of fissile material, a terrorist organization or rogue state could build one or more crude nuclear devices of the type used against Hiroshima. Approximately 25 kilograms of HEU could be enough to build one such bomb. Plutonium cannot be used to make a gun-barrel-type weapon like the Hiroshima bomb, but a small amount could be compressed by explosives to cause an explosion of a few kilotons — still very dangerous.

The risk is serious, and Russia presents the world's most pressing problem in this respect. A former Russian minister of atomic energy stated a few years ago that during the Cold War the Soviet Union had built 45,000 nuclear weapons and made enough fissile material for 90,000 more. It has been estimated that in 1990 the Soviet military maintained almost 22,000 nonstrategic nuclear weapons, and over 11,000 operational strategic weapons, with a comparable number in reserve, as well as an inactive stockpile.

In the aftermath of the Cold War, huge stockpiles of nuclear weapons and fissile material remained scattered throughout the former Soviet Union. The collapse of the Soviet Union and the economic and social disruption that followed in the successor states dramatically weakened controls over this enormous stockpile, which consists of hundreds of tonnes (1 tonne, or metric ton, equals 1,000 kilograms) of HEU and plutonium.

There are many ways that terrorists or rogue states might try to take advantage of the vast storehouse of nuclear bomb material that exists in Russia today. Nuclear material could simply be packed with a conventional explosive and used as a "dirty bomb" to spread radioactivity in urban areas. Or a nuclear weapon could be constructed using nuclear explosive material obtained by theft or illegal purchase from Russia. Such a device could be a gun-barrel type using HEU or a crude and inefficient implosion device using plutonium. To build a crude weapon of the Hiroshima type (of perhaps a 20-kiloton yield) using HEU might not be too difficult, although higher yields could be much more difficult; even a device of only several kilotons could be devastating in a large city. As Russia's nuclear weapons are reasonably well protected, there is a lesser risk that nuclear weapons could be stolen or illegally purchased. And, of course, one must consider the risk of the sale by North Korea of either a nuclear weapon or fissile material, or the diversion of a nuclear weapon in Pakistan, where there exists a stockpile of effective nuclear weapons amid a highly unstable and volatile political situation.

In 1991, anticipating this looming crisis, Senators Sam Nunn and Richard Lugar created the Cooperative Threat Reduction Initiative program known as the Nunn-Lugar program. This ambitious program undertook the reduction of the vast arsenal in Russia, and, over the years, impressive results were achieved (as reported by Rose Gottemoeller of the Carnegie Endowment in "Cooperative Inducements Crafting New Tools for Nonpro-

liferation," *Ultimate Security* 2003, pp. 127–28) Belarus, Kazakhstan, and Ukraine returned nearly 4,000 nuclear weapons to
Russia; more than 5,000 nuclear warheads have been deactivated
in Russia; a significant number of nuclear missiles has been
destroyed; and the first 100 tons of an agreed eventual 500 tons
of HEU have been purchased from Russia to be downblended to
low-enriched uranium to be consumed in nuclear power reactors producing electricity in the United States. However, it is clear
there is still a long way to go. Today, it is estimated that there remain
more than 1,000 tonnes of HEU and several hundred tonnes of
plutonium in the territory of the former Soviet Union. While
ninety-nine percent of this fissile material is located in Russia,
significant amounts still exist at civilian sites in Belarus, Kazakhstan, and Ukraine, as well as in Latvia and Uzbekistan. Roughly
half of the vast storehouse of nuclear explosive material in Russia is contained in the form of nuclear weapons, with the other
half scattered among some 400 buildings at more than fifty sites.

The Nunn-Lugar program began as an authorization to repro-
gram funds in the Department of Defense to do the work in the
former Soviet Union. After some years, the program received its
own direct appropriation, which has held steady at around $400
million a year. It has been joined by associated programs at the
Department of Energy (growing from $300 million a year to now
about $475 million a year), as well as a program of about $50 million a year at the Department of State to give nonweapon employ-
ment to Russian nuclear weapon scientists.

On January 10, 2001, a report prepared and submitted to the
outgoing Clinton administration by former Senate Majority
Leader Howard Baker and senior Washington lawyer Lloyd Cutler, who has long-standing ties to the national security establishment, warned in dire tones of the seriousness of this problem. They
recommended that the United States spend some $30 billion over
ten years, or $3 billion a year, to address this threat. It is worth

mentioning again that in fiscal year 2004, the United States plans to spend $9.1 billion on missile defense (with $10 billion proposed for fiscal year 2005) directed at one of the least significant of the strategic threats faced by the United States. At the same time, we are to spend less than $1 billion to address this most serious problem in Russia—and the administration has proposed a small reduction for 2005, despite positive words for the program by the president in his February 11, 2004, speech at the National Defense University.

Much has been accomplished, but vastly more needs to be done. Senator Lugar noted in a press release on February 11, 2004, that as "a consequence of the collapse of the Soviet totalitarian command and control society, a vast supermarket of weapons and materials of mass destruction became potentially accessible to rogue nations and terrorists." In their report, Senator Howard Baker and Lloyd Cutler state: "[T]he most urgent unmet national security threat to the United States today is the danger that weapons of mass destruction or weapons-usable material in Russia could be stolen and sold to terrorists or hostile nation states and used against American troops abroad or citizens at home. This is a clear and present danger to the international community" (A *Report Card on the Department of Energy's Nonproliferation Programs with Russia*, executive summary, p. iii).

The Nunn-Lugar Cooperative Threat Reduction program was signed into law in 1991. Since then, the Department of Defense, the Department of Energy, and the Department of State have been implementing the various programs developed pursuant to this legislation. These programs, managed separately, might have been more effective had they been centrally managed. There also was an assist to the Department of State in the spring of 2003 from a nongovernmental entity. The Nuclear Threat Initiative (NTI), founded by Ted Turner of CNN and led by former Senator Sam Nunn and former Deputy Energy Secretary, Charles Curtis, was asked by the department with little advance warning to provide the $5 million (which the Department of State did not have available at that time) necessary to seize an opportunity to acquire an amount of HEU associated with a research reactor in Belgrade. NTI quickly complied with the request.

From 1991 to 2002, the U.S. government spent approximately $7 billion on these programs, and, as indicated, approximately $1 billion was budgeted in 2004 for the programs for all three agencies. The Nunn-Lugar program initially focused on three primary areas: the destruction of nuclear and chemical weapons; the transportation, storage, disablement, and protection of nuclear weapons in the destruction process; and the establishment of safeguards against the spread of these weapons to other countries. As this program and related programs developed over time, with respect to the nuclear issue, they evolved into a comprehensive effort to deal with all aspects of nuclear weapons, nuclear explosive material, and nuclear technical expertise (that is, nuclear scientists) in Russia and in former Soviet states such as Ukraine and Kazakhstan. In addition to securing nuclear weapons and reducing their numbers, the objective of these programs is to reduce the existing amount of fissile material, reduce the size of the Russian nuclear weapon establishment, and reduce the incentive for Russian and Ukrainian nuclear scientists to move to other countries. As reported in the *Plan for Securing the Nuclear Weapons, Material and Expertise of the States of the Former Soviet Union*, submitted to Congress by the Department of Energy on February 3, 2003, key elements have included:

1. The reduction of nuclear explosive material. This involved reducing the production of plutonium for weapons by agreeing with the Russians that they will take steps to stop their plutonium production nuclear reactor. Also important here was an agree-

ment between the United States and Russia to eliminate part of their plutonium stockpiles. Another program was based on agreement between the United states and Russia to downblend up to 500 metric tonnes of Russian HEU from nuclear-weapon to reactor grade and sell the resulting low-enriched uranium to U.S. electric power utilities to be used in nuclear power reactors to produce electricity.

2. Maintaining the security of nuclear explosive material. This includes an elaborate program of security upgrades and improved record-keeping and accounting. Also part of this is a large storage facility for nuclear explosive material coming out of dismantled weapons at Mayak in the south Urals.

3. The reduction and security of Russian nuclear warheads. This includes upgrading storage and transportation security.

4. Reducing the size of Russia's nuclear weapon complex and inhibiting the outflow of Russian nuclear scientists to other countries, where they might help them learn to make nuclear weapons. This includes efforts to help Russian scientists enter the civilian economy as well as the construction of science centers to employ nuclear scientists in Moscow and in Kiev.

Nothing is more important than to eliminate as much as possible of this stockpile while we still can. Much has been accomplished under the Nunn-Lugar program, but the effort has only begun. Funding must be greatly increased; the relatively limited amount of funds set aside each year to address this desperately dangerous threat must change if we are to have security in the future. In January 2000, Senator Sam Nunn wrote on page seven of *Managing the Global Nuclear Materials Threat, Policy Recommendations*:

> The end of the Cold War and the dissolution of the Soviet Union brought many changes to the world, but none more important and hopefully more lasting than a reduction in the prospect of nuclear war between the two nuclear superpowers.

Yet the nuclear standoff that existed before the breakup had also provided a degree of stability, in that a confrontation that could lead to a nuclear clash between the United States and the Soviet Union presented risks clearly unacceptable to both.

Today, much of that stability has disappeared, replaced by new challenges of how to avoid the spread of nuclear weapons material and how to keep nuclear weapons out of the hands of terrorist groups and rogue nations. Again, we must do all that is possible to reduce these risks. . . .

Time is of the essence. We must act, and act now. But the United States cannot do it alone. Broad international cooperation . . . is essential. The consequences of failure are far too great and the risks too high to permit delay.

In March 2004, Senator Lugar wrote (in *Arms Control Today*, p. 4): "If we are to protect ourselves during this incredibly dangerous period, we must create new nonproliferation partners and aggressively pursue any nonproliferation opportunities that appear." The words of both these statesmen will likely remain valid and compelling for many years to come.

12

Regional Issues: Weapons of Mass Destruction in the Middle East and Nuclear Weapons in South and Northeast Asia

WEAPONS OF MASS DESTRUCTION, IN PAR-
ticular nuclear weapons, represent a worldwide problem, but three areas pose particular risks: the Middle East, South Asia, and Northeast Asia.

The political situation in the Middle East has been dominated for more than half a century by the conflict between the State of Israel and its surrounding Arab neighbors—particularly the Palestinians, who were displaced from their homes during the war for Israeli independence and who now live largely in adjacent areas that were seized from Jordan and Egypt by Israel during the 1967 war. This conflict is a principal cause of instability in the world today, is at the center of international security problems, and is used as justification for international terrorism. It simply must be resolved.

In the 1950s and 1960s, under a continuing threat of destruction by its neighbors, Israel began and developed a program to acquire a nuclear weapon capability. Israel was aided considerably by the French government, while the United States essentially looked the other way. By the late 1960s, Israel had developed a few workable atomic devices. Today, by some estimates, Israel possesses 100 to 200 sophisticated nuclear weapons that are deliverable in a few minutes to nearly every Middle Eastern capitol via their 1,500-mile-range Jericho II missile. Israel has consistently refused to join the NPT, which it could only do as a nonnuclear weapon state; all other states in the Middle East are members of the NPT. Israel possesses by far the strongest conventional armed forces in the region.

Egypt has a nuclear technology infrastructure, but has never pursued a weapon program. It does, however, have a chemical and biological weapon capability. Although Egypt has a peace treaty with Israel, it has profound misgivings about the Israeli nuclear weapon program, and in protest has refused to sign the Chemical Weapons Convention. Egypt was also reluctant to agree to a permanent NPT in 1995 for the same reason.

Syria has a chemical and biological weapon capability and a significant stockpile of these weapons. It also has refused to join the Chemical Weapons Convention.

Iraq, as is well known, had a rather advanced nuclear weapon program and was approaching the acquisition of a few crude nuclear weapons at the time of the first Gulf War. Iraq also had a vast chemical and biological weapon capability. The nuclear program was completely eliminated after the first Gulf War by the IAEA, and was not resuscitated. It now appears that the stocks of chemical and biological weapons were eliminated as well, but the capability to make such weapons may still exist, even after the 2003 conflict.

Iran has chemical and biological weapon programs, and—of more significance—appears to be moving toward a nuclear weapon capability while strongly asserting that it is interested only in civilian power production. Power reactors are being built for Iran by Russia that will produce spent fuel as part of the power production process, which, if not returned to Russia, could be reprocessed by Iran to produce plutonium. Iran is also building uranium-enrichment facilities, apparently at sites not declared to the IAEA and therefore in violation of their NPT-related IAEA safeguards obligations, perhaps with the purpose of making low-enriched uranium for power-reactor fuel, or, perhaps, for making HEU for weapons. However, after a strong intervention by the European Union, Iran has agreed to cooperate fully with the IAEA and "temporarily" suspend uranium enrichment activities. In late June, 2004 Iran gave notice that it would resume construction of centrifuges for uranium enrichment.

Libya, which reportedly some years ago tried to buy a nuclear weapon from China, decided in late 2003 to give up its weapons of mass destruction program, cooperate with the NPT and the IAEA, and join the NPT. This meant the elimination of its sizable chemical weapon capability and the destruction of its nascent nuclear weapon program. Libya had purchased centrifuges from the A. Q. Khan network in 1997 to enrich uranium, but this equipment never became operational. Apparently, Libya did not have scientists who knew what to do with this equipment, which has now been delivered to the United States. In 2001, North Korea reportedly delivered to Libya an amount of uranium, which if put through an enrichment process would have yielded enough HEU for one nuclear weapon. Apparently, the principal reason that Libya took the step of terminating its weapons of mass destruction program was to gain Western assistance for its flagging oil industry, although there may be more to it than that.

With ongoing religious hostility between Muslims and Jews in Palestine, the Middle East is one of the most volatile regions in the world, and the potential for conflict at present is still rising, not abating. The United States is present in Iraq amid turmoil, the Palestine situation remains dangerous and fragile, and the rise of Islamic fundamentalism in the region threatens governments everywhere. If the region is to know peace—indeed, if the world is to know peace and security—the Palestinian-Israel conflict needs to be resolved, and the world community must come to terms with the Middle East's desire not to be dominated by the West and to develop states that are democratic but at the same time Islamic. In this way the threat of violence by Islamic fundamentalism can be diminished.

As part of an overall settlement in the entire region, Middle East states should join the Chemical Weapons Convention and the Biological Weapons Convention, and Israel should take steps toward ultimately joining the NPT as a nonnuclear state once its security has been assured. This last step is important to peace in the Middle East, but it can only be accomplished in the context of a general Middle East settlement. To join the NPT, Israel would have to eliminate its nuclear weapons, but perhaps it could keep the nuclear explosive material on its territory under international safeguards as a hedge. There could also be a security guarantee from the United States, as well as assurance that no other state in the region would have a nuclear weapon program. Such a development would not only be in the interest of the world community but very much in the interest of Israel as well, which has the strongest army and the most advanced economy in the region. In the meantime and the foreseeable future, given the insecurities in today's world, Israel cannot be expected to give up its nuclear weapon program, but perhaps some other way for the medium term can be found to associate Israel (as well as India and Pakistan) with the NPT. This is important for the long-term viability of the treaty.

South Asia poses another problem, similar to the problem in the Middle East in that, in essence, the region's conflict evolves from a clash between religions (Islam versus Hindu) and the dispute focuses on a particular land area (the Indian state of Kashmir). But it differs in that both sides, Pakistan and India, are nuclear-armed states. India, which was formed in 1947 by the union of some 500 independent states, has refused to loosen its grip on Kashmir out of fear that to let one state go would risk losing others and the gradual dissolution of the Indian Union. Kashmir joined the Indian Union in 1947 by decision of its ruler, a Hindu maharajah, Hari Singh, the last independent maharajah of Kashmir; the overwhelming majority of the population then and now are Muslim, and would have preferred to be part of Pakistan. Thus, support of the Muslim population in Kashmir is essential to the survival of any government in Pakistan. In actuality, unlike in 1947, today most Kashmiris would probably prefer to have their own state, independent of both India and Pakistan.

This conflict reaches as far back into history as does the Arab-Israeli conflict. It began when the British departed in 1947, at the time of the partition of the British dominion of India, amidst great violence between the Indian Union and Pakistan. Three wars have been fought between India and Pakistan—the same number as between Israel and its Arab neighbors since the establishment of Israel in 1948. Almost as old as this confrontation is the Indian nuclear weapon program, which was first contemplated by Indian Prime Minister Jawaharlal Nehru to ensure great power status for India. This led to an Indian nuclear test in 1974, which was seen as a blow to the recently concluded NPT, and for which India was condemned by much of the world. Afterwards, India did not build weapons nor create a nuclear arsenal until after its round of five nuclear weapon tests in 1998. After this second testing of nuclear weapons, Indian Prime Minister Vajpayee left no doubt as to India's motivation: to give India the appearance of being a great power. India promptly proceeded to build a nuclear weapon stockpile and to develop missiles to deliver such weapons against Pakistan and eventually China.

The Pakistani nuclear weapon program began in 1965, when the first Pakistani research reactor began functioning. Pakistani

Prime Minister Ali Bhutto famously said at that time that if India should acquire nuclear weapons, Pakistan would have them as well even if the people had to "eat grass." He later noted that there was a Catholic bomb, a Protestant bomb, and a communist bomb—why not an "Islamic bomb"? In May 1998, following India's five nuclear weapon tests, Pakistan responded with six tests—its first. Thereafter, Pakistan began building nuclear weapons and, with Chinese help, developing missiles to deliver the weapons against India. However, it should be noted that Pakistan had already built nuclear weapons in the 1980s before it tested them—they were HEU-fueled and thus presumed reliable without testing. The actual tests in 1998 were therefore presumably a response to India rather than a design evaluation. The Pakistanis may also have worked on missiles prior to 1998. The Pakistani program developed a greater sense of urgency after the disastrous 1973 war with India, in which Pakistani forces were crushed by the Indian army and Pakistan was dismembered, with former East Pakistan becoming the independent state of Bangladesh.

India's weapons are plutonium weapons and Pakistan's are fueled by HEU. The weapons on both sides apparently have no safety devices, unlike U.S. and Russian weapons. Thus, if stolen by terrorists they could easily be used. Having fought three major wars and maintained a low-intensity conflict in Kashmir, the two sides remain more or less in a status of permanent alert. There were serious crises over Kashmir between the two countries in 1999 and 2002, when they were arming themselves with nuclear weapons. Because of the proximity of the two states, there is no warning time, thus, both sides have to keep their nuclear weapons on hair-trigger alert, ready to be launched on missiles at the slightest suggestion that the other side may have launched.

If nuclear war ever took place between Pakistan and India, millions would die. The United States and the Soviet Union successfully endured forty-five years of nuclear confrontation during the Cold War, but this should be of little comfort in contemplating the situation in South Asia. The United States and the Soviet Union had never fought a war against each other; Pakistan and India have fought three. The United States and the Soviet Union both had elaborate technical safety devices and other procedures to guard against accidental or unintended nuclear war; India and Pakistan have no such devices, although, like the United States and the Soviet Union, they have negotiated a number of useful nuclear confidence-building-measures, including dedicated and secure hotlines between the two governments. The heartlands of the United States and the Soviet Union are thousands of miles apart, providing considerable warning time to assess reports of possible missile launches. India and Pakistan are contiguous states with no warning time. Finally, in any case, the United States and the Soviet Union avoided nuclear war largely by luck. The situation between India and Pakistan cries out for some sort of negotiated nuclear arms control, but none has ever been considered. South Asia is truly the most dangerous place in the world today.

To add even more risk to this most dangerous situation is the ever-present risk of proliferation of nuclear weapons to terrorist organizations or rogue regimes, principally from Pakistan. With the Libyan decision to dismantle its nuclear weapon program came the revelation of the clandestine A. Q. Khan nuclear technology network. A worldwide organization based in Pakistan and led by the so-called father of the Pakistan nuclear weapon program, this underground network was revealed to have sold uranium enrichment technology and nuclear weapon designs to Libya, Iran, and North Korea. The Pakistan government received in turn from North Korea ballistic missiles that can deliver its nuclear weapons against India. So even though Pakistan has allegedly dismantled the Khan network, one can certainly agree with IAEA Director-General ElBaradei, who said in a February 5, 2004, press interview that the Khan case "raises more questions than it answers," represents only "the tip of the iceberg," that "we need to know who supplied what, when, to whom," and that "Dr. Khan was not working alone."

The third area of major crisis, Northeast Asia, presents a significantly different situation. North Korea, the last Stalinist communist state, with a failing economy and highly secretive in behavior, is determined to do anything to survive. To be more precise, its leadership, under dictator Kim Jong Il, is prepared to go to any lengths to survive. Pressured into the NPT as a nonnuclear state by the Soviet Union in the 1980s, it was years before North Korea finally agreed to the safeguards and inspections required by the treaty. It was operating a nuclear reactor during this period, and stopped its operation in the late 1980s long enough, perhaps, to extract sufficient spent fuel rods to reprocess the spent fuel and thereby acquire enough plutonium to possibly construct one or two nuclear weapons.

In 1992, U.S. satellites noticed two waste storage sites near the nuclear reactor, which, analysts believed, if inspected might reveal evidence that a diversion to nuclear weapon material had in fact taken place. The IAEA asked to inspect the two sites under its safeguards agreement with North Korea. This request was refused. The IAEA insisted and took the case to the Security Council of the United Nations. North Korea then announced it was giving the required ninety-day notice of withdrawal from the NPT, and the Security Council threatened sanctions. On the eighty-ninth day, at the end of March 1993, North Korea cancelled notice of its withdrawal from the NPT and agreed to negotiate with the United States. There followed a tense period of a year and a half with much strong rhetoric on both sides. During this time, North Korea withdrew some 8,000 spent fuel rods (containing enough plutonium for five to six nuclear weapons) from its nuclear reactor—against the express wishes of the United

States. The United States indicated that if the fuel rods were moved into the plutonium reprocessing facility nearby, the facility would be destroyed by U.S. cruise missiles. An official spokesman for North Korea replied that if the United States did this, it would turn the city of Seoul in South Korea into a "sea of fire."

After the visit of former President Jimmy Carter to North Korea in 1994, the two sides were able to come together and agree on a document called the Framework Agreement. Carter had been invited to come to North Korea in his capacity as head of the Carter Center, a private charitable organization in Atlanta that supports the causes of peace and human rights throughout the world. President Carter's trip was supported by the U.S. government with misgivings, but it was the turning point of the crisis and led to agreement. The Framework Agreement negotiated over some months provided that North Korea would terminate the operation of all of its nuclear facilities and that a Western consortium led by South Korea and Japan would build two large Western-style nuclear power reactors (which are more easily safeguarded) for North Korea. The United States would supply significant quantities of fuel oil to the North Korean economy (which, according to North Korea, would replace the power produced by the reactor to be shut down) and pledge not to threaten North Korea with nuclear attack. North Korea would stay in the NPT; the fuel rods would be continuously observed by IAEA inspectors; the existing nuclear reactor and the reprocessing plant would be shut down and placed under safeguards; and the IAEA would be able to inspect the two disputed waste storage sites when the two reactors to be built were about half complete. Finally, and most importantly to North Korea, there would be diplomatic relations between the United States and North Korea, and the United States would remove trade sanctions. The diplomatic recognition and security guarantee relate directly to North Korea's nuclear behavior. Normalization of relations with and the perceived absence of a military threat from the United States could have removed the incentive for North Korea to seek nuclear weapons.

The Framework Agreement operated successfully for a while, but, after many delays, the two reactors were never built. The United States was inconsistent in its provision of fuel oil, never lifted sanctions, and diplomatic relations were never established. The Clinton administration attempted to solve all of the outstanding issues with North Korea in 2000, but time ran out before this could be accomplished. The new administration decided not to pursue these nearly completed negotiations—largely, it seems, because they were a Clinton initiative—and included North Korea (along with Iran and Iraq) in its designation of the "Axis of Evil" in the president's State of the Union speech following the September 11 attacks. In 2002, the United States asserted that, in violation of the Framework Agreement and the NPT, North Korea had been secretly working on an alternate means of making nuclear weapons (by uranium enrichment). It was later learned in 2003 that the relevant technology had been supplied by the Khan network. As the United States began to prepare to invade Iraq in early 2003, North Korea dismissed the IAEA inspectors, withdrew from the NPT, restarted its nuclear reactor, and announced that it would reprocess the 8,000 spent fuel rods for plutonium and build nuclear weapons. The United States still refused to recommence direct negotiations with North Korea, saying it would not submit to "blackmail," and declared that it would only negotiate if other regional powers (i.e., China, South Korea, Japan, and Russia) were present. This remained the case into the summer of 2003, although one discussion meeting, which was considered a "regional" meeting due to the presence of China, was held in Beijing. In July of 2003, North Korea did agree to meet with the United States with the other four regional powers present. The meeting took place in Beijing in late August 2003, but recorded no progress, not even the scheduling of another meeting. By the fall of 2003, North Korea announced that it had completed reprocessing of the spent fuel and that it was building nuclear weapons and was nuclear capable. A second meeting was held in February 2004, with the United States and North Korea remaining far apart. By May 2004, there were newspaper reports stating that current intelligence estimates concluded that North Korea now had six to eight nuclear weapons. A third meeting took place in May 2004, which recorded no progress, but which was in part designed to prepare for a higher-level meeting in June. This meeting was held in late June 2004, and while it registered only limited progress, the United States, for the first time in this process, presented a comprehensive proposal termed "constructive" by North Korea. However, as indicated in Chapter 1, the United States stated that the two sides were still far apart.

With a long history of aggressive and provocative behavior, North Korea now appears to have acquired five or six nuclear weapons by reprocessing its fuel rods (in addition to the one or two weapons that they have may have had for some time). It also has an active program to build medium-range ballistic missiles. North Korea has sold medium-range ballistic missiles to Pakistan and Iran, and may have shared nuclear weapon technology with these two countries. Pakistan assisted North Korea with its uranium enrichment program. The prospect of the acquisition of nuclear weapons by North Korea is enormously dangerous to U.S. security and the security of its allies. North Korea could deploy the weapons on medium-range missiles and threaten South Korea and Japan (which would likely require some kind of test program for the weapons to reduce their size and weight so that they can be effectively carried by the North Korean missiles). Or it could sell weapons or plutonium (from which nuclear weapons could be easily made) to rogue states or to terrorist organizations such as Al Qaeda. This threat places every city in the world at risk. Yet, with 10,000 North Korean artillery pieces and rocket launchers backed by a one-million-man army deployed along the demilitarized-zone border between North and South Korea, less than 20 miles from Seoul, which is home to 14 million people, war is not the answer. North Korea could, in fact, turn Seoul into a "sea of fire" on short notice, with incalculable human costs. The only practical solution is U.S.-North Korean negotiations to give North Korea what it has said that it wants—diplomatic recognition and security—in exchange for what the United States wants—a verifiable end to North Korea's nuclear program. Let us hope that this is still possible.

13

America's Role

IN ADDRESSING THE THREATS OF TODAY'S WORLD, the United States has before it essentially two lines of approach. One path relies primarily on unilateral diplomatic pressure and, when necessary, preemptive military assault, in some cases without regard to existing treaty obligations or accepted international rules of behavior. Everyone agrees that there are some cases where such a policy is appropriate, such as the military action against Afghanistan following the terrorist attacks of September 11, 2001. But no one would argue that this should always be the path followed in dealing with a serious security threat. For example, with respect to alleged NPT violations by Iran, the United States has been working through established multilateral institutions such as the IAEA. There have been few voices urging military confrontation with Iran at this time.

The alternative path thus would be one which emphasizes international cooperation: developing and enforcing international treaty regimes such as the NPT and supporting multilateral institutions. Historically, the United States has been the architect and principal supporter of this approach to international order, and, as the country with the greatest stake in an international order built on treaty relationships, has been the most prominent champion of international law.

For over fifty years, the United States pursued a balance of power policy among the great powers—the United States, Russia, China, and Europe. The North Atlantic Treaty Organization and the U.S.-Japan alliance are among the institutions and partnerships created by this grand strategy, the centerpiece of which was containment of the Soviet Union, based on a nuclear deterrence policy which included negotiated arms restraint and which was designed to balance the forces of the two opposing camps. The United States pursued a world order built on rules and international treaties that permitted the expansion of democracy, the enlargement of international security, free market economies, and free trade. Within this international order, in addition to keeping the peace, the United States gave political cover to countries throughout the world to adopt the American position by joining international institutions and multilateral treaty regimes such as the International Telecommunication Union, the World Trade Organization, the Outer Space Treaty, the CFE Treaty, and the NPT.

However, in recent years the United States has moved away from this world system that it helped to create and toward a less cooperative and more unilateral and confrontational strategy. The United States has rejected new treaty arrangements important to key allies, such as the Kyoto Protocol on global warming and the International Criminal Court, instead of attempting to amend them or leave them quietly "on the shelf." For a long time, we refused direct negotiations with North Korea on their nuclear programs, and we have renounced treaty arrangements that are important to the world community, such as the Anti-Ballistic Mis-

sile Treaty and a verification and inspection annex to the Biological Weapons Convention.

John Ikenberry, a distinguished professor of geopolitics at
Georgetown University, referred to this new policy approach as
"neoimperial." In an article in the September–October 2002 issue
of *Foreign Affairs*, he stated that this new policy

> threatens to rend the fabric of the international community
> and political partnerships precisely at a time when that com-
> munity and those partnerships are urgently needed. It is an
> approach fraught with peril and likely to fail. It is not only
> politically unsustainable, but diplomatically harmful. And
> if history is a guide, it will trigger antagonism and resistance
> that will leave America in a more hostile and divided world.

An example would be the National Security Strategy document
of September 2002, in which the United States announced a policy of preemptive and preventive war against potential, but not
necessarily actual, threats from so-called rogue states and terrorist organizations. Over time, such a policy could strain our economy and our armed forces, and it appears to be wholly destructive
of the concept of the rule of law among the states of the world
community. A December 2002 addendum on strategy toward
threats involving nuclear, chemical, or biological weapons
(National Security Strategy to Combat Weapons of Mass Destruction) suggests that force, rather than cooperation and treaty
arrangements, is to be the principal means to combat the threat
of the proliferation of nuclear weapons and other weapons of mass
destruction.

Another example is the most recent Pentagon *Nuclear Posture
Review*, submitted in late 2001, which emphasizes the value of
nuclear weapons to the United States and implies that we might
use them against Iraq, Iran, North Korea, Syria, and Libya (con-

trary to our NPT pledge, as they were then all NPT nonnuclear weapon states), and also against Russia, as well as China (in defense of Taiwan). Combined with the National Strategy Document, this could create the impression that the United States might someday engage in preemptive or preventive war with the nuclear option on the table.

As evil, vicious, and corrupt as he was, Saddam Hussein was not the principal threat to the United States—or even a principal threat. Generals Norman Schwarzkopf and Wesley Clark, the military leaders in our previous two major wars, have made clear that the main threats to the United States are Al Qaeda and other international terrorist organizations, combined with nuclear proliferation. These must be our principal focus.

But how best to counteract this danger? Of course, increased vigilance and improved intelligence capabilities are essential. However, using the threat of force as the principal tool to combat proliferation of weapons of mass destruction, as implied by the White House strategy documents, can not and will not be the long-term answer. Military action can only do so much. The answer to the threat of catastrophic terrorism is social, political, economic, and diplomatic as well as military. In a larger sense, opposition to disease, poverty, and machine gun cultures around the world is as important to national security as military strength. We must be certain that in developing our policies, we are not unduly influenced by purely military considerations. These words from President Eisenhower's farewell address on January 16, 1961, are still relevant:

> In the councils of government, we must guard against the acquisition of unwarranted influence, whether sought or unsought, by the military-industrial complex.
>
> The potential for the disastrous rise of misplaced power exists and will persist. We must never let the weight of this

combination endanger our liberties or democratic processes. We should take nothing for granted. Only an alert and knowledgeable citizenry can compel the proper meshing of the huge industrial and military machinery of defense with our peaceful methods and goals, so that security and liberty may prosper together.

In deciding whether to pursue a unilateral or multilateral, diplomatic or military solution to a particular international crisis, the problem is not that any particular administration is wholly committed to one course or the other in advance. Obviously, each crisis, each problem has to be analyzed and judged on a case-by-case basis. Rather, the problem is the bias that any administration brings to a question. It is the United States' long-term commitment to multilateral institutions and the rule of law—or the lack thereof—that is important. Will the primary focus of the United States be to build an international system of interlocking treaty regimes and rules to promote international law and defeat aggression and terror, or will the United States place its trust primarily in a doctrine of preemptive war and an enormously capable military establishment? Both views have articulate proponents and most policy makers lean toward one course or the other. But what is to be emphasized? What is to be the bias?

This decision is a fateful one for the world as well as for the United States. The United States has been the most powerful country in the world for a hundred years. For a long time we chose not to use our power. We were late entering World War I, we did not join the League of Nations, and we were late entering World War II. We opposed colonial empires, and, for the most part, supported international law, open borders, and free trade, but remained isolated behind the two oceans that insulated us. With the close of World War II, however, this policy of isolation changed. The United States founded the United Nations, developed international economic institutions, promoted the NPT and many other international agreements limiting armaments, dismantled our army (the world's strongest in 1945), and did not immediately proceed to build a nuclear arsenal even though we had a monopoly after World War II.

But then came the Cold War, the long, gray struggle between freedom and tyranny that led to the creation of two enormous armed camps and huge stockpiles of nuclear weapons, and which inevitably caused the creation of two large industrial infrastructures to support this heavy investment in a standing military establishment. It also led to the increasing militarization of U.S. society, about which President Eisenhower expressed such grave misgivings.

Throughout the forty-five years of the Cold War, even though there was a military stand-off between the two superpowers, the United States was always the world's preeminent nation, without whose support little was possible. Now, with the collapse of the Soviet Union and the end of the Cold War, the United States is left as the sole surviving superpower—the world's only hyperpower, if you will. The future of the world is largely in our hands. Most diplomats and politicians around the world understand that without the United States in the lead, momentum for international initiatives usually disappears. We must use this power wisely. Unfortunately, other countries are complaining that instead of exhorting the faithful, the preacher himself needs to be reconverted. We are presently engaged in what is likely to be a long, sporadically violent, and dark struggle with the forces of international terrorism and disorder. The United States could choose to go it alone, to rely, when necessary, on the maintenance and quick deployment of our unique military power—the strongest the world has ever seen. But our strength is not limitless, and by failing to act through the world's system of institutions, treaty regimes, and rules, we risk arousing unnecessary opposition and discord in a world community that is almost entirely with us in the war against international terrorism and its associated rogue regimes.

In 1918, what is now Iraq and what is now Iran were made part of the British Empire—the largest empire in history. Even by 1922, it was clear that Britain had overreached. America does not need an empire. It needs peace, cooperation, and the rule of law. This is not a classic war of armies; rather, it is a subtle conflict of culture, economics, diplomacy, intelligence organizations, and sometimes of specially designed military forces. This is a war that can be won as long as the United States—and in the end it always has to be the United States—makes the right choices at the right times. America should return to its historic destiny of keeping the peace and fostering the development of the community of nations, democracies, free market economies, the international rule of law, international institutions, and treaty arrangements. This is both consistent with our principles and our national interest. It is in this way that the twin threats of nuclear proliferation and nuclear terrorism—in the end, the only way that the terrorists can defeat us—will be lifted. And it is in this way that the war on terror can and eventually will be won.

Conclusion

THE UNITED STATES IS THE STRONGEST
country in the world today, and the most significant to the
ultimate success of arms control and nonproliferation. The
American public usually supports arms control and the international rule of law (for example, a strong majority favor ratification
of the CTBT), but, as stated in the Introduction, apparently the
public does not consider these issues sufficiently important to
insist that U.S. political leaders either actively address them or
risk paying a political price. Thus many politicians believe themselves free to respond to the wishes of special interests rather than
those of the American people. If the United States and the world
community wishes to be secure in the future, this must change.

Perhaps the American public (and other publics) does in fact
consider these issues important. However, the issues may seem
so technical that only experts can understand them, and therefore elected representatives are relied upon to sort them out. But
in any country that functions as a representative democracy, it is

never wise to leave matters as important as these to elected representatives and government officials. In the end, arms control and nonproliferation are political issues and should be treated as such; policies made by political representatives must reflect the informed wishes of the people.

In a sense, these matters are highly technical and complex. But they are also simple, as I have attempted to express in this book. Do we want international peace and security issues to be determined by a system of rules and law or by force? Do we want to focus primarily on more and better weapons for our security? Or do we want to combine a strong defense with efforts to limit weapons so as to limit the potential destructiveness of conflicts? President Theodore Roosevelt famously declared that, in international affairs, the United States should "speak softly and carry a big stick." Are we to rely entirely on the "big stick"? Or will we consider "speaking softly" as well? The possibility remains, at least for now, of constructing a truly new world system based on international law and treaties. This potential world system represents perhaps the best chance history has yet given us to establish lasting peace, stability, and security for the world community.

This objective will not be easy to accomplish, and will greatly depend on effective and continuing international cooperation and consensus. In the course of building this consensus, there will need to be cooperation among states at many levels and respect for the views of all countries. Every country must commit to the international legal process and to the viability, strengthening, and expansion of international treaty regimes across the spectrum of issues affecting the global condition: security, environment, resources, health, economy, society, and so on. Each of these is vitally important, and security problems cannot be solved in isolation from them. If it is true that effective international policies in fields such as health and the environment require ever-increasing levels of cooperation among countries, surely this is just as true if not more so of the search for peace and stability in a dangerous world.

A case in point with respect to international cooperation is the NPT mentioned so often here. Some argue that traditional nonproliferation policies have already failed and that counter-proliferation (that is, the use of force rather than diplomacy and treaty regimes to inhibit proliferation) is the only viable policy. But traditional nonproliferation policies have not yet failed, and in the long term, international cooperation based on a shared commitment to international rules is the only way to win the war on terror. Of course, it will be difficult for traditional nonproliferation policies to succeed if the nuclear weapon states do not observe their part of the basic bargain, if the political value of nuclear weapons remains high, if rogue states pursue nuclear programs because they believe they are likely to be subject to military intervention, and if neighboring states are likely to respond to each other with nuclear weapon programs.

It has been clear for several years now that the choice is not between traditional nonproliferation and counter-proliferation policies, but rather between a strengthened and successful NPT regime and gradual descent into a widely proliferated world—one in which many states possess nuclear weapons and in which every conflict is a potential nuclear confrontation. The latter outcome would be very difficult to manage—even a minimum level of stability and security would be difficult to sustain. An effective NPT regime is still possible, but it will require great effort. It should be our dedicated objective.

Epilogue

IN COMBATING THE THREAT OF THE PROLIF-
eration of nuclear weapons and other weapons of mass destruction and the grave danger that these weapons may be acquired
by international terrorist organizations (as well as by rogue states),
it has been argued in these pages that military force is not the primary means whereby these threats can be successfully addressed.
Rather, to be effective, the response of the civilized world to the
threats of weapon proliferation and international terrorism must
largely be diplomatic, economic, and cultural in nature, with only
the occasional use of military force when necessary. Failed states,
regions of poverty and widespread deprivation, and machine gun
cultures are breeding grounds for international terrorism. These
problems cannot be solved by military force. Likewise, to prevent
the proliferation of nuclear weapons and other weapons of mass
destruction, the full cooperation of the world community is
essential. This is a diplomatic task. Such international cooperation is required in order to maintain a viable NPT regime, which

has been for thirty years and will continue to be the central instrument of international security in today's world.

The 9/11 Commission, in its report released on July 23, 2004, proposes important structural improvements, but also makes the point that we are in a war—not a war against an army, rather against an ideology. The report asserts the need to fight Al Qaeda and other elements of international terrorism with intelligence, military, economic, and diplomatic resources, but also argues that we need to emphasize our principles and values in our response to what has become an ideological war. Important in this effort, the report states, is that the United States "offer an example of moral leadership in the world . . . [and] abide by the rule of law" (p. 376).

A serving CIA officer, on July 19, 2004, anonymously published a book (approved for publication by the CIA) entitled *Imperial Hubris*. In this book, he asserts that we are losing the war on terror because we do not understand that it is our policies toward the Muslim world, not our values, that Al Qaeda is fighting. He suggests that we should consider modifying these policies, including our current position on the Palestine question and our support for tyrannical Muslim regimes. (He also notes that Al Qaeda "applauded" the U.S.-led invasion of Iraq in 2003 [p. 96].) The 9/11 report makes a comparable recommendation, emphasizing the issue of support for oppressive Muslim regimes, and recognizing the importance of improving cultural relationships.

Meanwhile, the North Korean nuclear weapon crisis continues without solution—a potential disaster waiting to happen— with a North Korean government spokesman referring to the U.S. offer made at the end of June as a "sham" (*New York Times*, July 25, 2004). The North Korean nuclear weapon program is a danger to the world community, both because of the possibility of direct use of such weapons and because of the potential of the sale of nuclear material to terrorist organizations.

There is a long struggle ahead of us, for which our tools will be primarily diplomatic, economic, and cultural. Treaty regimes and international law can play a central role in this struggle, just as they did in the Cold War. The 9/11 Commission report underlines the importance of abiding by the rule of law in our relations with other nations. By supporting treaty regimes and international law, the credibility of the United States will increase, making easier the crucial task of uniting the world community against the threat of nuclear terrorism. The more the international treaty system controlling nuclear weapons and other weapons of mass destruction can be strengthened, the less will be the risk of catastrophic proliferation, and the more the terrorists and their ideology will be isolated and opposed by a united world community. The cornerstone of this system is a viable and effective NPT regime. Strengthening this regime should be our highest priority.

Acknowledgments

PRESIDENT JOHN F. KENNEDY ONCE SAID, AND I paraphrase, "Success has many fathers; defeat is an orphan." Hopefully, this book will be a success, but in any case, it has many fathers and mothers. The idea for this book first arose in the aftermath of a speech I gave at the Seattle Civic Forum in the spring of 2003. As I was leaving, I stopped briefly at the table where my previous books, *Disarmament Sketches* and *Cornerstones of Security*, were being sold. The woman working the table said to me, "These books are all well and good, but you should write a book on this subject for the average person." With me at the time were Professor Chris Jones of the Jackson School at the University of Washington, Mark Leek of Pacific Northwest National Laboratory, and Michael Duckworth of the University of Washington Press, and they agreed that it seemed like a good idea. My wife, Christine, was very encouraging, and a few months later, after further consultations with Chris, Mark, and Michael, I decided to go ahead. This book is my attempt to be responsive to that original suggestion.

This book has been through many drafts. The first draft was

laboriously analyzed and edited by my stepdaughter, Missy Ryan, a former Reuters news correspondent in Peru, who contributed enormously to the creation of a much-improved second draft.

The first and second drafts were read, commented on, and significantly improved by Chris Jones's students as well as the staff of Pacific Northwest Laboratory in Seattle at Mark Leek's suggestion.

Chris Jones and Mark Leek reviewed the first three drafts and made many comments, almost all of which have been incorporated. Professor David Koplow of Georgetown University Law Center reviewed the third draft and was most supportive. Michael Duckworth at the University of Washington Press made steady improvements in the text throughout the process, and superb editing by Kerrie Maynes was a major factor. My son, Tommy, and my daughter, Elizabeth, helped with final draft proofreading and Tommy with the Epilogue. And Richard Rhodes provided some highly valuable technical contributions.

Lastly, the efforts of my assistant, Lesa Williams Richardson, made all of this possible by her tireless, highly capable, and consistent efforts in converting my words into readable script and bringing the book to its final form.

To all who have supported this project, I owe a great debt of gratitude. I hope the final product successfully represents their efforts and is a contribution to the ongoing national debate on this most important subject.

THOMAS GRAHAM JR.

Appendix 1

GLOBAL NUCLEAR STATUS

NPT Nuclear Weapon States	
United States	United Kingdom
Russian Federation	France
People's Republic of China	

Non-NPT Nuclear Weapon States *(able to deploy one or more nuclear weapons rapidly)*	
India	North Korea
Israel	Pakistan

High Risk States *(have not taken steps to acquire nuclear weapons)*	
Iran	

Abstaining Countries
(with the technological base but not the desire to build nuclear weapons; some have nuclear power plants subject to IAEA inspections)

Algeria	Ireland
Australia	Japan
Canada	Malta
Czech Republic	Mexico
Denmark	Norway
Egypt	Poland
Finland	South Korea
Germany	Spain
Hungary	Sweden
Indonesia	Switzerland
Italy	Taiwan*

* not recognized by the United States as an independent country

Renunciations

Algeria	Libya
Argentina	Iraq
Belarus	Romania
Brazil	South Africa
Kazakhstan	Ukraine

Source: Carnegie Endowment for International Peace

Appendix 2

TOTAL WARHEADS BUILT, 1945–2000

United States	70,000
Soviet Union	55,000
Britain	1,200
France	1,260
China	600
Total	128,060

Year	U.S.	Russia	Britain	FR	CH	Total
1945	2	0	0	0	0	2
1946	9	0	0	0	0	9
1947	13	0	0	0	0	13
1948	56	0	0	0	0	56
1949	169	1	0	0	0	170
1950	298	5	0	0	0	303
1951	438	25	0	0	0	463

Year	U.S.	Russia	Britain	FR	CH	Total
1952	832	50	0	0	0	882
1953	1,161	120	1	0	0	1,282
1954	1,630	150	5	0	0	1,785
1955	2,280	200	10	0	0	2,490
1956	3,620	400	15	0	0	4,035
1957	5,828	650	20	0	0	6,498
1958	7,402	900	22	0	0	8,324
1959	12,305	1,050	25	0	0	13,380
1960	18,638	1,700	30	0	0	20,368
1961	22,229	2,450	50	0	0	24,729
1962	27,100	3,100	205	0	0	30,405
1963	29,800	4,000	280	0	0	34,080
1964	31,600	5,100	310	4	1	37,015
1965	32,400	6,300	310	32	5	39,047
1966	32,450	7,550	270	36	20	40,326
1967	32,500	8,850	270	36	25	41,681
1968	30,700	10,000	280	36	35	41,051
1969	28,200	11,000	308	36	50	39,594
1970	26,600	12,700	280	36	75	39,691
1971	26,500	14,500	220	45	100	41,365
1972	27,000	16,600	220	70	130	44,020
1973	28,400	18,800	275	116	150	47,741
1974	29,100	21,100	325	145	170	50,840
1975	28,100	23,500	350	188	185	52,323
1976	26,700	25,800	350	212	190	53,252
1977	25,800	28,400	350	228	200	54,978
1978	24,600	31,400	350	235	220	56,805
1979	24,300	34,000	350	235	235	59,120
1980	24,300	36,300	350	250	280	61,480
1981	23,400	38,700	350	274	330	63,054
1982	23,000	40,800	335	274	360	64,769
1983	23,400	42,600	320	279	380	66,979
1984	23,600	43,300	270	280	414	67,864
1985	23,500	44,000	300	359	426	68,585

continued

Year	U.S.	Russia	Britain	FR	CH	Total
1986(*)	23,400	45,000	300	355	423	69,478
1987(*)	23,700	44,000	300	420	415	68,865
1988(*)	23,400	42,500	300	411	430	67,041
1989(*)	22,500	40,000	300	412	433	63,645
1990(*)	21,000	38,000	300	504	432	60,236
1991(*)	19,500	35,000	300	538	434	55,772
1992(*)	18,200	33,500	300	538	434	52,972
1993(*)	16,750	32,000	300	524	434	50,008
1994(*)	15,380	30,000	250	512	400	46,542
1995(*)	14,000	28,000	300	500	400	43,200
1996(*)	12,900	26,000	300	500	400	40,000
1997(*)	12,425	24,000	260	450	400	37,525
1998(*)	11,425	22,000	260	450	400	34,535
1999(*)	10,925	20,000	185	450	400	31,960
2000(*)	10,500	20,000	185	450	400	31,535

(*) U.S. (from 1988) and Soviet/Russian (from 1986) warheads include those in active, operational forces; retired, non-deployed warheads awaiting dismantlement; and weapons in reserve. For recent years, the estimate for the former Soviet Union/ Russia is 50 percent active, 50 percent retired/reserve.

Source: Robert S. Norris and William M. Arkin, "NRDC Nuclear Notebook, Global Nuclear Stockpiles, 1945–2000," *Bulletin of the Atomic Scientists*, March/ April 2000.

Appendix 3

WEAPON DEVELOPMENT MILESTONES

	United States	*U.S.S.R./Russia*
Warheads in stockpile (2003)	7,650 active, 3,000 reserve or awaiting disassembly	8,200 active, 10,000 reserve or awaiting disassembly
Peak number of warheads/year	32,500/1967	45,000/1986
Total number of warheads built, years	70,000 1945–1992	55,000 1949–2003
Atomic bomb developers	Leslie R. Groves, J. Robert Oppenheimer	Igor V. Kurchatov, Yuli B. Khariton, Boris L. Vannikov, Avraami P. Zaveniagin

continued

Hydrogen bomb developers	Stanislaw Ulam, Edward Teller, Richard Garwin	Andrei Sakharov, Yuli B. Khariton, Yakov B. Zeldovich
First operational ICBM	Oct. 31, 1959 Atlas D	Jan. 20, 1960 SS-6 Sapwood
First SSN enters service, vessel name	January 1955 Nautilus	August 1958 November
First SSBN patrol with Polaris-type SLBM, vessel, missile name	Nov. 15, 1960 G. Washington, Polaris A1	1968 Navaga/ Yankee, SS-N-6 Serb
First MIRVed missile deployed	Aug. 19, 1970 Minuteman III	Dec. 25, 1974 SS-18 Satan; April 26, 1975 SS-19 Stiletto
First warhead deployed without live nuclear test	B-61 Mod-11, 1996	unknown

	Testing milestones	
Number of nuclear tests/detonations	1,030/1,125	715/969
First fission test, type, yield	July 16, 1945 plutonium, 21 kt	Aug. 29, 1949 plutonium, 22 kt
First test of boosted fission weapon, yield	May 8, 1951 Item, 46 kt	Aug. 12, 1953 Joe 4, RDS-6c, 400 kt
First two-stage thermo-nuclear test, yield	Oct. 31, 1952 Mike, 10.4 Mt	Nov. 22, 1955 RDS-37, 1.6 Mt
Months from first fission bomb to first multistage thermo-nuclear bomb	87	75

Testing milestones (continued)

First nuclear airdrop, aircraft used, yield	Aug. 6, 1946 B-29, 15 kt	Oct. 18, 1951 Tu-4, 42 kt
Atmospheric tests, including underwater	215	219
Total Mts expended atmospheric/ underground	141/38	247/38
Largest atmospheric test, yield	Feb. 28, 1954 Bravo, 15 Mt	Oct. 30, 1961 50 Mt
Last atmospheric test	Nov. 4, 1962	Dec. 25, 1962
First underground test	July 26,1957	Oct. 11, 1961
Largest underground test, yield	Nov. 6, 1971 5 Mt	Oct. 27, 1973 2.8–4 Mt
Last test	Sept. 23, 1992	Oct. 24, 1990
Major test sites, (number of tests)	Nevada (901), Enewetak (43), Bikini (23), Christmas Island (24)	Semipalatinsk (456), Novaya Zemlya (130)
First computer-simulated test	2001, 12 teraflops White computer at LLNL, fully coupled primary and secondary explosion	unknown

continued

Nuclear infrastructure		
Assembly and disassembly plants	Pantex, near Amarillo, Texas	Avangard, Sarov (Arzamas-16), Lesnoy (Sverdlovsk-45), Trekhgorny (Zlatoust-36), Zarechny (Penza-19)

Source: Robert S. Norris and Hans M. Kristensen, "NRDC Nuclear Notebook, Nuclear Pursuits," *Bulletin of the Atomic Scientists*, September/October 2003.

Chronology

1945 The first nuclear test explosion is conducted in New Mexico on April 10.
   Hiroshima and Nagasaki are attacked with atomic bombs on August 6 and 9, respectively.

1946 The Cold War begins, recognized by Winston Churchill's "Iron Curtain" speech in Fulton, Missouri.

1948 Czechoslovakia is seized by the Soviet Union, signifying a major intensification of the Cold War.

1949 The Soviet Union tests its first atomic bomb.
   President Truman proposes a four-point program to help nations resist the advance of communism.
   The North Atlantic Treaty Organization (NATO) is founded.

1950 The United States conducts its first hydrogen bomb test explosion.

1952 The Soviet Union tests its first hydrogen bomb.
   Britain conducts its first nuclear weapon test.

1953 President Eisenhower delivers his "Atoms for Peace"

speech at the United Nations, which will lead to the
founding of the International Atomic Energy Agency
(IAEA) and the dispersal of peaceful nuclear technology
in an effort to head off weapon proliferation.

1954   The Soviet-dominated Warsaw Pact is founded.

1955   The first East-West summit meeting is held in Geneva,
Switzerland, and attended by the leaders of Britain,
France, the United States, and the Soviet Union.

1958–   U.S.-Soviet moratorium on nuclear weapon tests, which
61   the Soviet Union breaks in September 1961, with the
largest nuclear weapon test explosion of all time—more
than 58 megatons. A vigorous U.S. nuclear test series
follows.

1959   The first modern arms control treaty, the Antarctic
Treaty, is signed, among other things prohibiting nuclear
weapons in the Antarctic.

1960   France conducts its first nuclear weapon test.

1962   The Cuban Missile Crisis. In October, the United
States and the Soviet Union teeter on the brink of all-
out nuclear war, due to the secret basing of Soviet
medium- and short-range nuclear weapon missile systems
in Cuba. The crisis is resolved when the Soviets withdraw
the missiles and nuclear warheads in exchange for a U.S.
pledge not to invade Cuba and to later withdraw comparable U.S. medium-range nuclear weapon systems based
in Turkey.

1963   The Limited Test Ban Treaty (LTBT), the first major
East-West limitation on nuclear weapons, is signed by
the United States, the Soviet Union, and Britain.

1964   China conducts its first nuclear weapon test.

1967   The Outer Space Treaty is signed, banning the stationing
of nuclear weapons or other weapons of mass destruction
in outer space.

A U.S.-Soviet summit meeting is held in Glassboro, New
Jersey, which will lead to the commencement of the SALT
negotiations two years later.

The Treaty of Tlatelolco is signed, banning nuclear weapons in Latin America.

1968   The Nuclear Non-Proliferation Treaty (NPT) is signed.

1969–   The Strategic Arms Limitation Talks (SALT I) culminate
72   in the signing of the Antiballistic Missile (ABM) Treaty and the Interim Agreement on Strategic Offensive Arms in 1972.

1970   The United States deploys its first multiple independently targetable reentry vehicle (MIRV) system, by which one strategic nuclear missile can strike many targets.

The NPT enters into force.

1972   The ABM Treaty and the Interim Agreement are signed.

The Biological Weapons Convention (BWC) is signed.

1972–   The SALT II negotiations are held, culminating in the
79   signing of the SALT II Treaty in 1979.

1975   The Soviet Union deploys its first MIRV systems.

The Helsinki Final Act is signed and goes into effect.

1979   The Soviets invade Afghanistan.

The NATO two-track decision on medium-range nuclear systems is agreed upon in December. The decision is to attempt to resolve the Soviet medium-range nuclear missile threat to Europe within four years by arms negotiations, and failing that, to deploy new U.S. medium-range nuclear weapon missile systems in Europe.

The SALT II Treaty, a comprehensive agreement between the United States and the Soviet Union limiting strategic offense, is signed.

1981   The Intermediate-Range Nuclear Forces Treaty (INF) negotiations on medium-range nuclear weapon missile systems in Europe commence. President Reagan proposes that all such systems be eliminated (the "zero-option") even though at that time the Soviet Union had 1200 medium-range nuclear weapon missile systems deployed against Europe and the U.S. had none deployed in Europe against the Soviet Union.

The Convention on Certain Conventional Weapons (CCW) is signed.

1982   The Strategic Arms Reduction Talks (START) negotiations commence.

1983   The Soviets walk out of the INF and START negotiations because of the commencement of U.S. deployment in Europe of Pershing II and ground-launched cruise missile (GLCM) medium-range nuclear weapon missile systems in accordance with the 1979 NATO decision. President Reagan announces in March the Strategic Defense Initiative (SDI), which could place strategic defense systems in outer space.

1984   The Soviets shoot down Korean Airlines KAL-007, with a U.S. Congressman on board, over the Sea of Japan. This is the lowest point of the Cold War.

1985   Nuclear arms control negotiations resume in Geneva as the Nuclear and Space Arms Negotiations, comprising three subnegotiations: INF, START, and outer space. The Treaty of Rarotonga is signed, establishing a nuclear-weapon-free zone in the South Pacific.

1986   The Helsinki summit meeting is held between Presidents Reagan and Gorbachev in October, following the Geneva summit meeting of December 1985. It is a watershed meeting, although, because of SDI, it fails to achieve a comprehensive arms control solution. The zero-option solution for INF systems and, more importantly, the principle of intrusive on-site inspections to verify this agreement are agreed upon.

1987   The INF Treaty is signed.

1989   The Conventional Armed Forces in Europe (CFE) negotiations begin. The Berlin Wall collapses and communist governments throughout Eastern Europe are overthrown. The Soviets withdraw from Afghanistan.

1990   The CFE Treaty is signed, effectively ending the Cold War.

1991   The START I Treaty is signed, reducing strategic nuclear
        weapon systems for the United States and the Soviet
        Union to 6,000 each.
        On December 25, the Soviet Union collapses, leaving
        twelve successor states in its wake, including Russia,
        Ukraine, Belarus, and Kazakhstan, with strategic nuclear
        weapon systems on their territories.

1992   The Lisbon Protocol is signed, substituting Russia,
        Ukraine, Belarus, and Kazakhstan as parties to the
        START I Treaty in place of the Soviet Union. It is agreed
        that Russia will become a party to the NPT as a nuclear
        weapon state, in place of the Soviet Union, and that
        Ukraine, Belarus, and Kazakhstan will join the NPT
        as nonnuclear weapon states.

1993   The START II Treaty is signed by the United States and
        Russia, reducing strategic nuclear weapon systems to
        3,000 to 3,500 for each party.
        The Chemical Weapons Convention (CWC) is signed.

1993–   The first nuclear weapon crisis with North Korea, which
94   threatens to withdraw from the NPT. The crisis is resolved
        by negotiations between the United States and North
        Korea, culminating in the 1994 Agreed Framework,
        whereby North Korea agrees to remain in the NPT and
        dismantle its nuclear weapon program in exchange for
        diplomatic relations, a security guarantee and economic
        incentives from the United States and the West's promise
        to build North Korea two Western-style nuclear power
        reactors.

1994   START I enters into force, with a seven-year reduction
        period to 6,000 strategic nuclear weapons each for the
        United States and Russia.

1995   The NPT is indefinitely extended.
        The Treaty of Bangkok is signed, establishing a nuclear-
        weapon-free zone in Southeast Asia.

1996   The Comprehensive Nuclear Test Ban Treaty (CTBT) is
        signed.

The Treaty of Pelindaba is signed, establishing a nuclear-weapon-free zone on the African continent.

1997   An agreement to START III principles, including the reduction of strategic nuclear weapon systems to 2,000 to 2,500 for each side, is reached at a Clinton-Yeltsin summit meeting.

1998   India and Pakistan conduct nuclear weapon tests and announce that they consider themselves nuclear weapon states (although no one else does).

1999   The fiftieth anniversary of NATO. Agreement on the first NATO expansion, taking in Hungary, Poland, and the Czech Republic as new members.

The CTBT is rejected by the U.S. Senate (ratified by Britain, France, and Russia between 1998 and 2000).

2000   The NPT Review Conference. All NPT parties (which by then included all but four countries in the world—Cuba, India, Pakistan, and Israel) agree to the "unequivocal" commitment to the elimination of nuclear weapons, a continued moratorium on nuclear weapon testing pending entry into force of the CTBT, and that the ABM Treaty is "the cornerstone of international security" (Cuba later joined the NPT, and in 2003 North Korea withdrew).

2001   Al Qaeda terrorists attack New York City and Washington, D.C., on September 11.

The United States gives the required six-months' notice of intent to withdraw from the ABM Treaty.

The United States and Russia announce that the Start I Treaty reductions have been completed.

2002   The United States withdraws from the ABM Treaty.

The Treaty of Moscow is signed, calling for the reduction of strategic nuclear offensive weapons in operational status to 1,700 to 2,000 by the United States and Russia in ten years (by December 31, 2012).

The START II Treaty (and START process) is abandoned.

2003   North Korea withdraws from the NPT and announces the resumption of its nuclear weapon program.

In March, Iraq is invaded by the United States and Britain. In August, the United States, North Korea, China, Russia, South Korea, and Japan meet in Beijing on the North Korean nuclear issue. No progress is achieved.

In December, Iran admits to violations of its NPT safeguards agreement with the IAEA and agrees to cooperate with the IAEA in the future, including intrusive inspections and to "temporarily" suspend its construction of uranium-enrichment facilities.

In December, Libya announces its decision to eliminate its chemical weapon program and nascent nuclear weapon program. In the process, the A. Q. Khan network based in Pakistan is disclosed, which has been secretly selling nuclear weapon technology to Iran, Libya, and North Korea for years.

2004   In February, a second meeting is held in Beijing on the North Korean nuclear issue. Again, no progress is achieved. In May a third meeting is held in Beijing to prepare for a high-level six-power meeting in June. This meeting is held in late June, and while only limited progress is made, for the first time in the process the Unites States advances a comprehensive proposal which the representative of North Korea terms "promising."
In late June, Iran formally announces the resumption of construction of uranium-enrichment facilities.

Glossary

ABM: Anti-ballistic missile

ABM Treaty: Anti-ballistic Missile Treaty. Formally known as
Treaty between the United States of America and the Union
of Soviet Socialist Republics on the Limitation of Anti-ballistic
Missile Systems. Signed and entered into force in 1972 at the
conclusion of the first Strategic Arms Limitation Talks (SALT
I), the ABM Treaty limited the deployment of national missile
defenses by either the United States or the Soviet Union (now
Russia) and, pursuant to a 1974 protocol, limited each side to
one ABM deployment site. The treaty was intended to stabilize
nuclear deterrence between the superpowers, thereby facilitat-
ing strategic arms limitations and reductions. The United
States gave notice of withdrawal to Russia under Article XV
(the six-month withdrawal clause) on December 13, 2001,
and formally withdrew on June 13, 2002.

active defenses: The deployment of devices intended to deflect,
destroy, or render unworkable offensive weapons.

Additional Protocol: This IAEA protocol was the response to the call for improved NPT verification in the Statement of Principles and Objectives. It was opened for signature in 1997. By 2004 only about 20 percent of NPT states parties had signed and ratified it.

Al Qaeda: A worldwide terrorist organization founded by Osama Bin Laden that has declared war on the United States. This organization was responsible for the September 11, 2001, attacks on New York City and Washington, D.C., and many other terrorist attacks.

Antarctic Treaty: Signed in 1959 and entered into force in 1961, the Antarctic Treaty prohibited the testing of nuclear weapons or the conduct of any measures of a military nature in Antarctica, thus preserving the continent as a nonmilitarized, nuclear-weapon-free area.

anthrax: A well-known disease caused by bacteria spores. The most dangerous form of the disease, pulmonary anthrax, is also a favored biological weapon agent.

Anti-ballistic Missile Treaty: *See* ABM Treaty.

arms race stability: A term normally used to refer to a situation in which strategic defense is kept to a low level, thereby removing the incentive to build more strategic offensive systems to overcome defenses.

ballistic missile: A missile system designed to operate on the basis of ballistic technology, as does a bullet. In the case of strategic missiles, this means that after launching a missile beyond the Earth's atmosphere, its return to the Earth and striking of the target are propelled by the force of gravity. As strategic ballistic missiles reenter Earth's atmosphere and approach their targets, they reach enormous speeds, and are accompanied by decoys; as a result, they are nearly impossible to defend against.

Baruch Plan: The plan presented in 1946 to the UN by financier Bernard Baruch on behalf of the United States designed to internationalize nuclear technology. It was rejected by the Soviet Union.

basic bargain: The central deal enshrined in the NPT, whereby most of the world (the nonnuclear weapon states parties) agreed never to acquire nuclear weapons and to accept treaty safeguards on their peaceful nuclear activities (Articles 2 and 3) in exchange for the commitment of the five nuclear weapon state parties (the United States, Britain, Russia, France, and China) to share peaceful nuclear technology (Article 4) and engage in nuclear disarmament negotiations aimed at the ultimate elimination of nuclear weapons (Article 6).

Biological Weapons Convention (BWC): Formally known as Biological Weapons Convention on the Prohibition of the Development, Production, and Stockpiling of Bacteriological (Biological) and Toxin Weapons and on their Destruction. The BWC, which opened for signature in April 1972 and entered into force in 1975, required parties not to develop, produce, stockpile, or acquire biological agents or toxins "of types and in quantities that have no justification for prophylactic, protective, and other peaceful purposes," as well as biological weapons and means of delivery.

boost phase system: A missile defense system designed to intercept ballistic missiles during the lift-off phase of flight.

botulinum toxin: A highly poisonous chemical and favored biological weapon produced by the bacteria which causes botulism.

B-29 bomber: A World War II strategic bomber.

calculated ambiguity: The doctrine of reserving all of one's military retaliatory options, but implying a possible nuclear weapon response under certain circumstances.

CCW: *See* Convention on Certain Conventional Weapons.

CEP: Circular error probable. A means of measuring the accuracy of a ballistic missile. The CEP is the radius of a circle within which 50 percent of the warheads deployed on a specific missile type are projected to fall.

CFE Treaty: Treaty on Conventional Armed Forces in Europe. Signed in 1990 and entered into force in 1992, the CFE Treaty set limits on the number of major units of combined arms (including battle tanks, armored combat vehicles, artillery pieces, combat aircraft, and attack helicopters) that the states parties may deploy in Europe (between the Atlantic and the Ural Mountains).

Charter of the United Nations: The founding document of the United Nations.

Chemical Weapons Convention (CWC): Opened for signature in 1993 and entered into force in 1997, the CWC prohibits the acquisition of chemical weapon agents and chemical weapons "in any circumstances," provides for the destruction of existing stocks, and has an elaborate verification system that includes regulated on-site inspection. The CWC has nearly 150 parities.

circular error probable: *See* CEP.

Cold War: The era of worldwide hostility between the United States and the Soviet Union from 1946 to 1991, marked by thermonuclear confrontation between the two superpowers.

Comprehensive Nuclear-Test-Ban Treaty: *See* CTBT.

Conference on Disarmament: A standing UN-related organization located in Geneva, Switzerland, established for the purpose of negotiating arms control agreements. Originally called the Ten Nation Disarmament Committee (designed to bring together East and West), it later became the Eighteen Nation Disarmament Committee, then, due to further expansion, the Conference of the Committee on Disarmament, and now for some years the Conference on Disarmament. The CTBT, NPT, BWC, CWC, and the Seabed Arms Control treaties were negotiated at this forum, which operates by consensus and currently consists of 66 member nations.

confidence-building measures: Negotiated transparency measures to include on-site inspections, stationing of observers, and exchange of information designed to enhance military and political stability.

Convention on Certain Conventional Weapons (CCW): Formally known as Convention on Prohibitions or Restrictions on the

Use of Certain Conventional Weapons Which May Be Deemed
to Be Excessively Injurious or to Have Indiscriminate Effects,
the CCW opened for signature in 1981 and entered into force
in 1983. It has four protocols limiting specific weapons (fragmentation weapons, incendiary weapons, land mines, and laser
weapons, which are separately signed and ratified.

counter-proliferation: The use of military force and other forms
of pressure, such as economic sanctions, in place of treaty
regimes and diplomacy to impede and prevent the proliferation
of nuclear weapons and other weapons of mass destruction.

crisis stability: This term usually refers to a situation whereby,
as a result of strategic defense being kept to a low level, the
incentive to strike first with strategic offensive arms in a crisis
is reduced because the effectiveness of a retaliatory strike with
strategic nuclear weapons is assured.

cruise missile: A missile similar to a small, pilotless airplane, in
that it operates on the basis of aerodynamic lift and flies at
very low altitudes. It carries a highly accurate guidance system
on board.

CTBT: Comprehensive Nuclear-Test-Ban Treaty. Opened for signature in 1996, the CTBT banned all nuclear explosions and
established an extensive International Monitoring System to
verify compliance with its provisions. As of July 2004, it had
been signed by 172 nations and ratified by 114, but it cannot
enter into force until 44 specified states (those members of
the Conference on Disarmament that have nuclear facilities
on their territory) have ratified. As of the same date, 41 of these
have signed and 32 have ratified.

Cuban Missile Crisis: The confrontation between the United
States and the Soviet Union in 1962 over the secret deployment
by the Soviet Union of nuclear weapons and missiles in Cuba,
which very nearly escalated into all-out thermonuclear war.

customary international law: Composed of international law rules
which have existed sufficiently long and which have been recognized by a large enough number of states to be considered to

have passed into an international common law binding on all nations. An example is the Geneva Protocol that now binds all nations, whether parties or not.

CWC: *See* Chemical Weapons Convention

dirty bombs: Nuclear explosive devices made with spent reactor fuel, with little or no explosive power, but which can release a great deal of radiation.

executive agreements: Lower-level international agreements that can establish international legal commitments (but not domestic law, as in a treaty) and which usually enter into force upon signature.

final document: In this book, the negotiated and agreed formal document concluding an international conference.

fissile: Capable of undergoing nuclear fission.

Framework Agreement: Formally known as the Agreed Framework Between the United States of America and the Democratic People's Republic of Korea, the Framework Agreement was signed in 1994 and became effective upon signature. It settled the 1993–94 nuclear crisis with Korea.

freeze agreement: In this book, refers to an agreement prohibiting increased numbers of strategic nuclear weapon systems.

Geneva Protocol: Formally known as Protocol for the Prohibition of the Use in War of Asphyxiating, Poisonous or Other Gases, and of Bacteriological Methods of Warfare. Opened for signature on June 17, 1925 and entered into force on February 8, 1928, the Geneva Protocol bans the use in war, but not the production or possession, of chemical and biological weapons. With reservations taken by many parties, it is considered to be a ban on the first use in war of chemical and biological weapons. The U.S. Senate approved the protocol on December 16, 1974, and it entered into force for the United States on April 10, 1975.

Glassboro Summit: At this meeting in Glassboro, New Jersey, in June 1967, the first discussion of strategic arms limitations took place. President Lyndon B. Johnson, Soviet Prime Minister Aleksey Kosygin, and their diplomatic and military advisors met to discuss Arab-Israeli tensions in the Middle East following the Six Day War of June 1967, U.S.-Soviet arms limitations, and the prevention of the proliferation of nuclear weapons.

gun-barrel technology: *See* gun bomb.

gun bomb: The type of atomic bomb exploded over Hiroshima, where one piece of nuclear material is simply fired up the barrel of a small cannon to mate with a second piece fixed to the cannon's muzzle, forming a supercritical assembly and starting a nuclear chain reaction. A simple and rugged but highly inefficient design, typically requiring three or four times as much HEU as an implosion bomb, and unsuitable for plutonium.

Helsinki Final Act: Formally known as Final Act of the Conference on Security and Cooperation in Europe, the Helsinki Final Act was signed in 1975 and became effective upon signature. In addition to extensive provisions on international borders and human rights in Europe, it also provided for prior notification of military exercises involving more than 25,000 troops, and for exchanges of observers during such maneuvers.

Helsinki Framework Agreement: The 1997 summit agreement between Presidents William Clinton and Boris Yeltsin to extend the reduction deadlines of the START II Treaty by treaty amendment and to negotiate a START III Treaty lowering the strategic offensive arms levels to between 2,000 and 2,500 systems.

Helsinki Process: The follow-on process to the 1975 Helsinki Final Act, which led to a vast array of confidence-building measures, human rights initiatives, and arms control agreements in Europe, contributing greatly to stability. Included among these were the CFE Treaty and the 1986 Stockholm Document.

HEU: Highly enriched uranium. Natural uranium (which consists of 99.3 percent uranium-238 and 0.7 percent uranium-235) enriched in its rarer isotope to weapons' grade, above 80 percent U-235, making it suitable for use in nuclear explosives and as fuel for small, powerful nuclear reactors such as those used in nuclear submarines.

highly enriched uranium: *See* HEU.

IAEA: International Atomic Energy Agency. A United Nations–related organization promoting the peaceful uses of atomic energy and guarding against its destructive use.

ICBM: Intercontinental ballistic missile. Defined in the SALT II treaty as having a range in excess of 5,500 kilometers (3,440 miles).

IMS: *See* International Monitoring System.

INF Treaty: Formally known as Treaty between the United States of America and the Union of Soviet Socialist Republics on the Elimination of their Intermediate-Range and Shorter-Range Missiles. Signed in 1987 and entered into force in 1988, the INF Treaty is the only treaty to eliminate an entire class of nuclear-weapon delivery vehicles (ground-launched ballistic and cruise missiles with ranges of between 500 and 5,500 kilometers or 310 and 3,440 miles).

Interim Agreement: *See* SALT I.

intercontinental ballistic missile: *See* ICBM.

International Atomic Energy Agency: *See* IAEA.

International Court of Justice: World court located in The Hague in the Netherlands. Part of the United Nations system.

international humanitarian law: Part of customary international law that includes rules regulating armed conflict and features the rule of proportionality and the requirement that weapons not be indiscriminate as to civilian casualties.

International Monitoring System (IMS): System established pursuant to the CTBT to enhance efforts to monitor possible international nuclear explosive test activities.

International Strategy Conference: Conference held in Ottawa in October 1996 to begin negotiations on a treaty banning anti-personnel land mines.

International Telecommunications Union: The international treaty regime which regulates the worldwide use of radio frequencies.

Kara Sea seismic event: A 1997 underwater earthquake beneath the Arctic Ocean north of Russia, near the former Russian nuclear test site on the Arctic island of Novaya Temla.

Khan network: The secret and illegal network that for many years supplied nuclear weapon technology and design information to Libya, Iran, and North Korea. Headed by the "father" of the Pakistani nuclear weapon program, Dr. A. Q. Khan.

kiloton: The equivalent in explosive power of 1,000 tons of TNT.

Limited Test Ban Treaty: *See* LTBT.

Lisbon Protocol: Signed in Lisbon in 1992 and entered into force with the START Treaty in 1994, this protocol multilateralized the START I Treaty by adding Belarus, Kazakhstan, Russia, and Ukraine as parties in place of the Soviet Union.

Little Boy: The name given to the atomic bomb dropped on Hiroshima in 1945.

long-range nuclear missile forces: Nuclear-capable missiles with ranges of over 3,440 miles (5,550 kilometers) and therefore considered strategic offensive weapons.

low-enriched uranium: Nuclear-power-reactor-grade uranium enriched in U-235 to less than 20 percent (usually around 3 or 4 percent).

LTBT: Limited Test Ban Treaty. Formally known as Treaty Banning Nuclear Weapon Tests in the Atmosphere, Outer Space, and Under Water. Signed and entered into force in 1963, the LTBT banned nuclear explosions underwater, in the atmosphere, and in outer space. It also banned underground nuclear explosions if radioactive debris from any such explosion would cross national borders.

MAD: Mutually assured destruction. The Cold War nuclear deterrence relationship between the United States and the Soviet Union, based on the threat of overwhelming retaliation in the event of an attack with nuclear weapons.

megaton: One thousand kilotons, the equivalent in explosive power of one million tons of TNT.

MIRV: Multiple independently targetable reentry vehicle. A MIRVed ICBM is an ICBM with several warheads, each capable of being aimed and released toward a separate target.

Missile Technology Control Regime: See MTCR.

MTCR: Missile Technology Control Regime. An informal group of some thirty-plus industrialized nations established in 1987, much like the Nuclear Suppliers Group, formed to control the export of ballistic missile technology with specific agreed export limitations.

multiple independently targetable reentry vehicle: See MIRV.

mustard gas: A highly toxic poison gas which causes severe blistering on the skin and severe and often fatal damage to the mucus lining of the lungs.

mutually assured destruction: See MAD.

M-X (Peacekeeper) missile: A modern and highly accurate ICBM, the M-X missile was the subject of such controversy in the 1980s that only 50 were ever deployed in silo launchers, and never in the originally planned mobile mode.

National Security Council: The U.S. government cabinet-level committee which addresses national security issues, chaired by the president.

National Security Strategy to Combat Weapons of Mass Destruction: A policy document published by the Bush administration in December 2002 specifically applying U.S. strategy—including the doctrine of preemptive military attack—against the threat of weapons of mass destruction potentially coming into the possession of hostile states and organizations.

National Security Strategy: Formally known as National Security Strategy of the United States of America. A document published by the Bush administration in September 2002, best known for its promulgation of a U.S. doctrine of preemptive military action against hostile states and organizations which may threaten the United States.

NATO: North Atlantic Treaty Organization.

negative security assurances: NPT-related undertakings by the NPT nuclear weapon states not to attack NPT nonnuclear weapon states with nuclear weapons (unless attacked by such a state in alliance with a nuclear weapon state).

no-first-use policy: An undertaking not to initiate the use of nuclear weapons or introduce nuclear weapons into any future conflict, and limiting any use of nuclear weapons to retaliation to a nuclear weapon attack by another state.

nonnuclear weapon state: A party to the NPT, other than the five accepted nuclear weapon states, that has agreed never to acquire nuclear weapons.

NORAD: North American Aerospace Defense Command. Military command system originally created to protect the North American continent from bomber attack, it later evolved into a system for early warning of missile attack.

North American Aerospace Defense Command: *See* NORAD.

North Atlantic Treaty Organization: *See* NATO.

NPR: *Nuclear Posture Review.* A periodic review of U.S. nuclear policy prepared by the Department of Defense. The most recent review was completed in December 2001.

NPT: Nuclear Non-Proliferation Treaty. Formally known as Treaty on the Non-proliferation of Nuclear Weapons, the NPT opened for signature in 1968, entered into force in 1970, and was indefinitely extended in 1995. In exchange for a commitment from the nonnuclear weapon states parties (today numbering 182 nations) never to develop or otherwise to acquire nuclear weapons and to submit to international safeguards intended to verify compliance with this commitment, the nuclear weapon states—the United States, the Soviet Union (now Russia), Britain, France, and China—promised unfettered access to peaceful nuclear technologies and pledged to engage in disarmament negotiations aimed at the ultimate elimination of their nuclear arsenals.

NPT Review and Extension Conference: The conference held in 1995, twenty-five years after entry into force of the NPT, according to the terms of the treaty, to determine the duration of the NPT. The conference agreed to indefinitely extend the NPT.

NTI: Nuclear Threat Initiative. A nongovernmental organization founded by Ted Turner of CNN, the NTI works largely on nuclear nonproliferation issues. Former Senator Sam Nunn is the chairman and Charles Curtis, former Deputy Secretary of Energy, the president.

nuclear deterrence: A doctrine developed during the Cold War to minimize the risk of nuclear war that depended on a secure second-strike capability to deter nuclear attack.

Nuclear Non-Proliferation Treaty: See NPT.

Nuclear Planning Group: The NATO nuclear policy committee.

Nuclear Posture Review: See NPR.

Nuclear and Space Arms Negotiations: The U.S.-Soviet strategic arms negotiations of the 1980s, which led to the INF and START I treaties.

Nuclear Suppliers Group: A group of around forty industrialized nations which have agreed to limit the export of dual-use goods related to the development of nuclear weapons.

Nuclear Threat Initiative: See NTI.

nuclear umbrella: Protection by the deterrence capability of U.S. nuclear weapons for nations allied to the United States (i.e., NATO, Japan, and South Korea). Also known as "extended deterrence."

nuclear weapon state: A state with nuclear weapons integrated into its national arsenals and ready for use.

Nunn-Lugar program: Formally known as Cooperative Threat Reduction Initiative program, the Nunn-Lugar program was established by Senators Sam Nunn and Richard Lugar to earmark a small portion of the national defense budget to help finance the security and eventual elimination of excess nuclear weapons and nuclear bomb material as well as chemical and biological weapons and agents in Russia and other successor states of the Soviet Union left over after the Cold War.

Ottawa Convention: Formally known as Convention on the Prohibition of the Use, Stockpiling, Production, and Transfer of Antipersonnel Mines and on Their Destruction, the Ottawa Convention opened for signature in 1997 and entered into force in 1999.

Ottawa Process: The process ultimately sponsored by the Canadian government, which led to the successful negotiation of the Ottawa Convention.

Outer Space Treaty: Formally known as Treaty on Principles Governing the Activities of States in the Exploration and Use of Outer Space, Including the Moon and Other Celestial Bodies, this treaty opened for signature in 1967 and entered into force in 1967. Based on the principles of the Antarctic Treaty, it banned the establishment of military facilities on any heavenly body (such as the moon) and prohibited the orbiting around the Earth or otherwise stationing in space of nuclear weapons or other weapons of mass destruction. A preambular clause provided that outer space was to be used exclusively for peaceful purposes.

Patriot missile: A U.S. short-range anti-ballistic interceptor missile deployed during the first Gulf War that displayed only limited effectiveness.

P-5: The five permanent members of the UN Security Council: China, France, Russia, Britain, and the United States. Also the five nuclear weapon states recognized by the NPT.

plutonium: A man-made element (element 94) that is more than twice as fissile as HEU (q.v.) and that chain-reacts. It is bred in nuclear reactors, after which it can be separated chemically from the spent fuel. In its pure form, like HEU, it is only mildly

radioactive, making it an excellent fuel for fission weapons
as well as for the fission primaries of hydrogen bombs.

Review and Extension Conference: Formally known as Review
and Extension Conference of the Parties to the Treaty on the
Non-Proliferation of Nuclear Weapons. The 1995 conference
of NPT parties that completed a regular five-year review and
also agreed to indefinitely extend the NPT.

rogue states: Commonly used phrase meaning hostile, unstable
states—the prime example today being North Korea.

rule of proportionality: Rule providing that in warfare it is contrary
to law to respond to an armed attack with significantly greater
force than is necessary to repel and defeat the attacker.

safeguards agreement: The NPT verification system administered
by agreement of each party with the IAEA.

Safeguard missile defense system: The ABM system deployed by
the Nixon administration to protect ICBM deployment areas,
limited to one site by the ABM Treaty.

SALT: Strategic Arms Limitation Talks. The first negotiation,
sometimes referred to as the SALT I negotiations, took place
from 1969 to 1972, and the second negotiation, sometimes
called the SALT II negotiations, took place from 1972 to
1979.

SALT I: Formally known as The Interim Agreement Between the
United States of America and the Union of Soviet Socialist
Republics on Certain Measures with Respect to the Limitation
of Strategic Offensive Arms. Signed and entered into force
in 1972, SALT I expired by its terms in 1977, but was informally
extended until terminated in 1986. It placed limits on the number of strategic offensive nuclear delivery missile systems the
Soviet Union and the United States could deploy. It essentially
froze the parties where they were.

SALT II: Formally known as The Treaty Between the United States
of America and the Union of Soviet Socialist Republics on the

Limitation of Strategic Offensive Arms. SALT II was signed in June 1979, but never entered into force. It would have placed specific limits on U.S. and Soviet strategic offensive nuclear delivery systems, including heavy bombers, but the accord was never ratified by the United States, although it was informally observed from signature to a point in 1986 some months beyond its expiration date of December 31, 1985.

SCUD: An early ballistic missile system based on the German World War II V-2 rocket.

SDI: Strategic Defense Initiative. The program developed under President Ronald Reagan to defend against the Soviet ICBM force. It never got beyond the research phase. Nicknamed "Star Wars" by opponents.

Seabed Arms Control Treaty: This 1972 treaty prohibits the placing of nuclear weapons or other weapons of mass destruction on the beds of international waters beyond the twelve-mile limit.

sea-launched cruise missile: A long-range cruise missile launched from ships and submarines. The nuclear version is considered part of strategic offensive forces.

SORT: Strategic Offensive Reductions Treaty. Signed in 2002 and entered into force in 2004, this treaty reduces "operationally developed strategic nuclear warheads" to a total of between 1700 and 2200 by December 31, 2012. These weapons are not required to be eliminated and may be kept in storage.

special session on disarmament: The first of several UN special sessions on disarmament was in 1978. At this meeting, the United States, Britain, and the Soviet Union pledged not to use nuclear weapons against nonnuclear weapon states party to the NPT (unless they conduct an attack in alliance with a nuclear weapon state).

START: Formally known as Strategic Arms Reduction Talks. The first series of these negotiations, from 1981 to 1991, is sometimes referred to as the START I negotiations and the second, from 1992 to 1993, as the START II negotiations.

START I: Formally known as The Treaty Between the United

States of America and the Union of Soviet Socialist Republics on the Reduction and Limitation of Strategic Offensive Arms, START I was signed in 1991 and entered into force in 1994. It required Russia and the United States to reduce their strategic nuclear arsenals to 6000 deployed warheads. This objective was officially reached in December 2001.

START II: Formally known as The Treaty Between the United States of America and the Russian Federation on Further Reduction and Limitation of Strategic Offensive Arms. START II was signed in January 1993, but never entered into force. It would have required Russia and the United States to reduce their strategic nuclear arsenals to between 3000 and 3500 deployed warheads.

Statement of Principles and Objectives: Formally known as the Statement of Principles and Objectives for Nuclear Nonproliferation and Disarmament. This statement of arms control commitments was agreed upon at the 1995 NPT Review and Extension Conference, and was designed to strengthen the nonproliferation regime and (politically if not legally) condition the extension of the NPT.

states parties: Members of a treaty regime.

Stockholm Document: Formally known as the Document of the Stockholm Conference on Confidence- and Security-Building Measures and Disarmament in Europe Convened in Accordance with the Relevant Provisions of the Concluding Document of the Madrid Meeting of the Conference on Security and Cooperation in Europe, this document was signed in 1986 and became effective upon signature.

stockpile confidence tests: Tests conducted on currently deployed weapons to confirm their reliability.

Stockpile Stewardship Program (SSP): The Department of Energy program designed to maintain the reliability and safety of the U.S. nuclear stockpile without conducting nuclear explosive tests. Currently funded at around $5.5 billion.

Strategic Arms Limitation Talks: See SALT.

Strategic Arms Reduction Talks: See START.

Strategic Defense Initiative: *See* SDI.

strategic defensive systems: Anti-ballistic missile systems designed to defend against long-range nuclear missiles (strategic ballistic missiles).

strategic nuclear forces: Land-based long-range ballistic missiles (with ranges in excess of 5500 kilometers, or 3440 miles), submarine-launched ballistic missiles, and heavy bombers with nuclear weapons. Later, long-range nuclear-capable cruise missiles were added to this force.

Strategic Offensive Reductions Treaty: *See* SORT.

strontium 90: A radioactive byproduct of atmospheric nuclear explosive testing, which found its way into the food chain throughout the world and thereby provided a strong impetus to the negotiation of the LTBT.

submarine-launched ballistic missile: A long-range nuclear-capable ballistic missile launched from a submarine.

Taepodong I rocket: A North Korean three-stage ballistic missile based on SCUD technology, which some feared to be an incipient ICBM. So far, it has been tested only once.

theater missile defense: Defense of U.S. troops and allies overseas against shorter-range missiles.

Treaty of Bangkok: Treaty establishing a nuclear-weapon-free zone in Southeast Asia. The treaty was opened for signature in 1995 and entered into force in 1997.

Treaty on Conventional Armed Forces in Europe: *See* CFE Treaty.

Treaty of Moscow: *See* SORT.

Treaty of Pelindaba: The African Nuclear Weapon Free Zone Treaty. Opened for signature in 1996, it has not yet entered into force. This treaty would establish a nuclear-weapon-free zone covering the land area of the African continent.

Treaty of Rarotonga: The South Pacific Nuclear Weapon Free Zone Treaty. This treaty was opened for signature in 1985 and entered into force in 1986. It established a nuclear-weapon-free zone in the land area of the South Pacific.

Treaty of Tlatelolco: The Treaty for the Prohibition of Nuclear

Weapons in Latin America. This treaty was opened for signature in 1967 and by 2002 it had entered into force for all Latin American states, but only became effective in 2004, as some Latin American countries only recently signed their IAEA Safeguards agreement (a requirement for full treaty effectiveness). This treaty would establish a nuclear-weapon-free zone consisting of the land area (and adjacent ocean areas) of the Western Hemisphere south of the U.S.-Mexican border.

Vienna Convention: Formally known as the Vienna Convention on the Law of Treaties. An international agreement on international law applicable to treaties. The United States has not ratified the convention, but recognizes the substantive provisions (as opposed to the procedural rules), in the convention as reflective of customary international law and therefore binding on all states.

Vienna documents: A series of confidence-building agreements providing for an exchange of information on military forces stationed in Europe.

v-2 rocket: A World War II–era early ballistic missile system.

Warsaw Pact alliance: The Soviet-sponsored counterpart to NATO, which, in addition to the Soviet Union, included East Germany, Czechoslovakia, Hungary, Poland, Romania, and Bulgaria. It collapsed shortly before the end of the Cold War.

weapons of mass destruction: Nuclear, chemical, and biological weapons and their delivery systems.

World Court: *See* International Court of Justice.

World Trade Organization: The current international organization of the world's trading countries. A very high percentage of the world's states are members. China has recently joined, and Russia is trying to join.

Index